ARCO

Literary Critiques

Byron

Francis M. Doherty

arco

New York

Published 1969 by ARCO PUBLISHING COMPANY, Inc.
219 Park Avenue South, New York, N.Y. 10003
Copyright © Francis M. Doherty, 1968, 1969
All Rights Reserved
Library of Congress Catalog Number 72-78856
Printed in the United States of America

Arco Literary Critiques

Of recent years, the ordinary man who reads for pleasure has been gradually excluded from that great debate in which every intelligent reader of the classics takes part. There are two reasons for this: first, so much criticism floods from the world's presses that no one but a scholar living entirely among books can hope to read it all; and second, the critics and analysts, mostly academics, use a language that only their fellows in the same discipline can understand.

Consequently criticism, which should be as 'inevitable as breathing'—an activity for which we are all qualified—has become the private field of a few warring factions who shout their unintelligible battle cries to each other but make little communication to the common man.

Arco Literary Critiques aims at giving a straightforward account of literature and of writers—straightforward both in content and in language. Critical jargon is as far as possible avoided; any terms that must be used are explained simply; and the constant preoccupation of the authors of the Series is to be lucid.

It is our hope that each book will be easily understood, that it will adequately describe its subject without pretentiousness so that the intelligent reader who wants to know about Donne or Keats or Shakespeare will find enough in it to bring him up to date on critical estimates.

Even those who are well read, we believe, can benefit from a lucid exposition of what they may have taken for granted, and perhaps—dare it be said?—not fully understood.

K. H. G.

Contents

Acknowledgements

The author and publishers are indebted to John Murray for permission to reproduce the engraving by George Henry Harlow of Byron in 1818 on the cover and for the drawing of Byron in 1823 by Count Alfred d'Orsay. The engraving of Newstead Priory is reproduced by courtesy of the City Librarian of Nottingham and the Curator of Newstead Abbey.

Byron

George Gordon Lord Byron, the sixth of the title, has always fascinated biographers (and he has many), though his poetry has tended to be rather more neglected by the critics. This is not to say that his life, a most romantic one by anyone's standard, is more entertaining than his writing. It is not as simple as that. There are, perhaps, three Byrons. There is the Byron of the letters and journals, spirited, racy, energetic, and full of warmth, wit and liveliness (what he calls, at one point, his 'allegrezza'). There is the Byron of the poems most popular in his own time, a handsome, misanthropic, cursed and blighted being, doomed to destruction, and magnetically, mysteriously attractive to all who meet him. Then there is the Byron of the last great poems, notably *Don Juan*, a major satirist and a real poetic inventor, writing uniquely compelling verse which surveys modern man and his plight with an experienced, sardonic but compassionate eye. So this makes it difficult to start even with the simple 'life' and 'work' opposition, because each of the three Byrons can appear in the same place side by side and not feel uncomfortable; though the point about 'life' and 'work' as contenders for one's interest is a false one in Byron's case anyway. The work so closely follows and is modelled on the life that many critics have been led to treat the poetry as autobiographical source material. Though there is danger in this, there is at least this important truth: Byron could write only from actual experience. He had little faculty for fiction, though, on the other hand, a good facility in reproducing actual incident and emotional mood. For a Romantic poet Byron was often far too hard-headed and far too prosaic really to be counted with the other English Romantic poets. For an artist he had surprisingly little sensitivity towards or understanding of the other arts: his knowledge of music was slim, though he liked rather trite and simple ballads; his response to painting and sculpture was negligible, and so on. This will only be one of the many paradoxes and contradictions the critic has calmly to swallow; there are many more. F. M. D.

Byron (Genoa 1823). From a drawing by Count Alfred d'Orsay.

A New Vision by Robert Southey. This is a parody of Southey's poem and a violent attack on him as an ex-Jacobin, on George IV and on the Ministers.

A Noble Poet—Scratching up his Ideas by Williams. Byron's later work is shown as being influenced by the Devil ('Old Scratch'), particularly *The Vision of Judgement* published in *The Liberal*, October 1822.

Newstead Priory, Nottinghamshire. From an engraving published
October 1779 of a painting by Paul Sandby, R.A.

I

Byron's Life

Byron was born on 22 January 1788, at 16 Holles Street in London, son of the former Scottish heiress, Catherine Gordon of Gight, and the improvident and impecunious Captain ('Mad Jack') Byron. Both families were startling, aristocratic, and renowned for deeds of violence and their tangled fortunes. The father had already, at the age of twenty-two in 1778, met and conquered the rather splendid Lady Carmarthen, whose husband was to be the fifth Duke of Leeds, and had created a scandal followed by a divorce by Act of Parliament. Of the three children of that marriage only one survived, Augusta, the future poet's beloved half-sister, born in 1783.

Having disposed of the £23,000 of his second wife in quick time, Captain Byron lived a life of dodging creditors, and left his wife and baby in financial hardship. The baby had been born with a caul and with a deformed right foot, 'a conventional clubbed foot, the heel being drawn up and the sole of the foot being turned inwards'. The next year mother and son went to live in Aberdeen, where, with a nurse, Agnes Gray, they lived modestly on the mother's remaining annual £150.

Young George's formal education was conventional and rudimentary, but he read all that he could get his hands on, travels, histories and novels, and the Bible. He particularly enjoyed the Old Testament which he read with his Calvinist nurse, thereby laying in for life the notion of predestination, the possibility of being doomed by God to eternal punishment.

This 'dooming' is so important in Byron's future life that one ought to say how much Byron felt that idea being reinforced by his reading outside the Bible. An obscure novel by John

Moore, *Zeluco*, for example, is referred to by Byron in his preface to the first two cantos of *Childe Harold's Pilgrimage*: 'the outline which I once meant to fill up for him [Harold] was, with some exceptions, the sketch of a modern Timon, perhaps a poetical Zeluco'. The novel shows us a misanthropic hero–villain, doomed by forces beyond his control to do evil. Equally, one might gather from the frequency with which Byron's mind, working at speed and without premeditation in his letters, returns to Shakespeare's *Macbeth* for illustrative quotation, that the hero–villain who does evil almost unwillingly, under pressure from forces outside himself, was a favourite emblem of his own state of mind. One could say that *Macbeth* had a fascination for Romantic poets, and that Shelley was another notable example, as his juvenile romances show close if crude affinities with the play (as Bernard Blackstone shows in *The Lost Travellers*).*

Byron became heir-presumptive to the barony by the death of the grandson of the 'Wicked Lord' Byron in battle in Corsica on 31 July 1794, but no help or friendship came from the Wicked Lord, now an old man heavily in debt and closeted in Newstead Abbey, the ruined baronial seat in Nottinghamshire, with his tame crickets, memories and sorrows. Finally, on 21 May 1798, the old Lord died, leaving a tangled mass of legal encumbrances, heavy debts and a ruinous estate for the new master. Nonetheless, the mother and son moved into the gloomy and romantic Abbey.

Byron's life now expanded: he spent holidays in London with his lawyer's family, the Hansons, and he went to Harrow in April 1801, as befitted his new station, staying until 1805. There he fought his way through the taunts at his lameness, provoking his teachers, neglecting his lessons, and managing to become the ringleader of a faction opposing the appointment of a new Headmaster. His school friendships were passionate and remained especially strong in memory.

He met his half-sister, Augusta, sometime in this period, and was writing to her in 1804 and finding someone to whom he could boldly unburden himself of his growing and impassioned dislike of his mother.

---

*Or as G. Wilson Knight has amply studied for Byron alone in his *Byron and Shakespeare* (Barnes & Noble, New York).

The climax of his Harrow days was playing in the Eton and Harrow cricket match in Dorset Square, London, on 2 August 1805. He says he made 11 and 7 runs (Wisden's *Almanack* says 7 and 2), and he was extremely proud of his ability to play games, despite his lameness and despite his having to have a runner for the match.

Cambridge followed in October, and he entered Trinity College with one of the most liberal allowances in College, £500. He indulged himself, spent lavishly, got into the hands of money-lenders, involved himself deeply with other men, and generally amused himself. The friendships with men show a homosexual tendency exhibited throughout his life, and this was noted by his lifelong friend, John Cam Hobhouse. We might note, for example, the friendship with the Cambridge choirboy, John Edlestone:

> His *voice* first attracted my attention, his *countenance* fixed it, and his *manners* attracted me to him for ever. . . . I certainly love him more than any human being, and neither time nor distance have the least effect on my (in general) changeable disposition. . . . He certainly is perhaps more attached to *me* than ever I am in return. During the whole of my residence at Cambridge we met every day, summer and winter, without *one* tiresome moment, and separated each time with increasing reluctance. . . . He is the only being I esteem, though I *like* many.
>
> LETTERS AND JOURNALS I, 133–5. 5 July 1807

In 1811 Edlestone was dead, and this was to be one of several blows to Byron in the same year, profoundly disturbing him and inclining him more and more to think that he was a doomed being, bringing disaster to all who came close to him. This 'violent, though *pure*, love and passion' produced several verse items in *Fugitive Pieces* of December 1804, notably 'To E' and 'The Cornelian'.

His life, however, was not confined to Cambridge. He lived high in London (mainly on borrowed money), forming friend-ships and liaisons with all manner of people, high and low, and experimenting with living. He negotiated his first slim volume of verse with John Ridge, a printer at Newark, and this appeared as *Fugitive Pieces* in November 1806. The Reverend Thomas Becher who had been sent a copy by Byron so objected to some of the erotic poems that Byron recalled the edition and burned all the copies (though four copies did survive the flames). He chastened his verse, and *Poems on Various Occasions,* the volume's new title, appeared in January 1807. About 100 copies were printed, and Byron later changed some twenty items for more melancholic ones, to republish the book as *Hours of Idleness.*

In 1808 he established himself in London and began to cultivate friendships, dissipations, pugilists and verse. He toyed, too, with the notion of escaping from England for 'a view of the Peloponnesus and a voyage through the Archipelago . . .', as he wrote to his friend De Bathe. But while still in England he suffered at the hands of the *Edinburgh Review* which savaged the *Hours of Idleness.* This organ of literary propriety was also a Whig paper, Byron's own political persuasion, and Byron was affronted on both counts. He wrote to Hobhouse on February 27:

> As an author, I am cut to atoms by the E[dinburgh] Review; it is just out, and has completely demolished my little fabric of fame. This is rather scurvy treatment for a Whig Review, but politics and poetry are different things, and I am no adept in either. I therefore submit in silence.
>
> LORD BYRON'S CORRESPONDENCE, ed. John Murray, 1922, I. p. 2

Of course, he did not submit in silence. He started a satire which was to form the nucleus of the poem published in 1809 as *English Bards and Scotch Reviewers,* though by then there were to be other enemies to snap up in it.

In March 1808 he got copies of the re-worked *Hours of Idleness,* now appearing as *Poems Original and Translated.* He had cut out the preface which had so offended the *Edinburgh Review* and several of the more trivial poems, adding five poems which heightened the nostalgic regret for the passing of boyhood. The collection was scornfully reviewed by the Cambridge man Hewson Clarke in *The Satirist,* no doubt as part of a campaign against Byron which had started by Clarke printing some of the adverse criticism of Byron's verse in May, and then following with a poem in June, 'Lord B——n to his Bear'. Byron had gone to Cambridge that summer to receive his M.A. degree and was incensed at Clarke. He had indeed kept a bear in college and had caused a sensation by taking it for its exercise on a lead and by saying that it was sitting for a fellowship, but his anger was not simply at the ridicule that Clarke was pouring on him. One imagines that there must have been the feeling of failure, the lack of achievement, because he fell into a deep depression and gloom at this time, though it must be remembered that he had been playing havoc with his physical constitution with his London excesses, both Gargantuan and debilitating.

In September Byron was back at Newstead, thinking over his plans for his projected journey, furnishing rooms and building up his new satiric poem with the help of the *Epistle to Peter Pindar* and the *Baviad* of Gifford, the editor of the Tory *Quarterly Review* and a harsh, slashing satirist. Hobhouse was with him a good part of the time but went off at the end of November, leaving Byron alone and rather bored with himself until he set off for London in January 1809. He took with him the manuscript of the poem, now *The British Bards*, and was eager both for its publication and for his entrance into the House of Lords. Byron's guardian, Lord Carlisle, whom Byron intended to celebrate in his poem as a 'new Roscommon' on whom 'Apollo deigns to smile', treated him coldly and did not offer to introduce him formally to the House. Accordingly, when he had settled on the final title for the poem, *English Bards and Scotch Reviewers*, he impaled his guardian:

> Lord, rhymester, petit-maître, pamphleteer!
> So dull in youth, so drivelling in his age,
> His scenes alone had damn'd our sinking stage.

He was to add to his vituperation over the next edition both in text and footnote, but this would do for now.

The manuscript was entrusted to Robert Charles Dallas, a distant relative, who had introduced himself to Byron in a fawning way in January 1808, and Dallas found a publisher who put out a thousand copies of the poem. It appeared just after

Byron had, in a coldly disdainful manner, taken his seat in the House on March 13. The poem sold well, despite its anonymity, and it was felt to be by Byron, but the author had left town for a final visit to Newstead and his mother with a party of cronies for a wild time at the Abbey. When he heard how the poem was selling, Byron hurried to town and was there on April 25; of course, he also wanted to escape from England as quickly as he could. However, the money for the trip was not forthcoming from the lawyer, Hanson, and he had to postpone his departure initially until June. During the period of waiting he spent some time in preparing a second edition in which he would sting Jeffrey, the man whom he thought the writer of the attack in the *Edinburgh Review*, and would maul Hewson Clarke of *The Satirist*.

He was delayed until July 2, mostly by lack of finances, and was saved eventually by Scrope Davies who lent him £4800 which he had won gambling. He set off with Hobhouse, whom he was financing, and a German, Friese, who had seen service in Persia. They sailed on the Lisbon Packet from Falmouth in gay spirits.

> Now at length we're off for Turkey,
> Lord knows when we shall come back!
> Breezes foul and tempests murky
> May unship us in a crack.
> But, since life at most a jest is,
> As philosophers allow,
> Still to laugh by far the best is,
> Then laugh on—as I do now.
> 'Lines to Mr. Hodgson Written on Board the Lisbon Packet'
> 30 June 1809

Almost two years were to be spent abroad in Spain, Greece and the Near East. Spain enthralled him and he stayed nearly a month; Gibraltar he found dirty and detestable and left after a fortnight for Malta. Here he fell in love with a Mrs. Spencer Smith, an 'everlasting passion' as he wrote later in 1812 to Lady Melbourne, and the attachment lasted a month with a promise to meet again in Malta. On to Greece, after being involved in a challenge to a duel (on Mrs. Smith's account), landing at Preveza. He set out for Jannina, the capital of the renowned Ali Pasha, an exciting and dangerous journey. The rugged mountains, the barbaric splendour, the mellow-mannered butcher of a Pasha all burnt themselves into Byron's memory, and all were to be recalled in various ways in the Oriental Tales.

On Christmas Day he was in Athens, and soon after his arrival he finished the first canto of *Childe Harold's Pilgrimage* which he had started on 31 October. He enjoyed his stay immensely, and a trip to the furthest point of Attica gave him a sight of the 'Isles of Greece', a vision of such power and beauty that his imagination was haunted by it all his life. On 5 March he left Athens, its carnival, its agreeable climate, its engaging people and Theresa Macri (who becomes 'The Maid of Athens') for Turkey.

On his journey he performed on 3 May the feat he was proudest of: he swam across the Hellespont, the feat that legendary Leander achieved to reach his beloved Hero. Every letter home was full of self-congratulations, and he also marked the exploit with verse, a very good lyric (one of his few) marrying disenchanted romanticism to a real speaking voice. The last two stanzas can serve as representative:

> But since he cross'd the rapid tide,
>   According to the doubtful story,
> To woo,—and—Lord knows what beside,
>   And swam for Love, as I for Glory;

> 'Twere hard to say who fared the best:
>   Sad mortals! thus the gods still plague you!
> He lost his labour, I my jest;
>   For he was drown'd, and I've the ague.

One naturally compares verse of this sort with *Childe Harold*, the second canto of which he had finished in March, and sees that the natural voice is what characterises the smaller verse, what links it to the Byron of the letters, and, more importantly, to the later Byron of *Don Juan*.

Life in Turkey was limited, so he returned to Athens in

August to a Capuchin monastery at the foot of the Acropolis, living in a little world of his own with even a small library. Low life, the study of Italian with a young and devoted friend, Nicolo Giraud, the writing of *Hints from Horace*, a long poem satirising contemporary authors (a more classical *English Bards and Scotch Reviewers*), all filled his time, and a letter from Mrs. Spencer Smith, faithful to the tryst in Malta, was only a dead voice to him now. But he had to leave, and, very reluctantly, he did, on 22 April 1811.

He landed in Malta, stayed a month in low spirits, to which Mrs. Spencer Smith's presence added more gloom, and suffered from poor health and fever, the oppressive heat and the thought of England. England meant creditors who had to be faced, and utter financial chaos.

There he came on July 11, a cosmopolitan, a man with a great deal of varied experience and the foundation of a worldly wisdom, with the sun in his bones and for whom the Mediterranean had become 'the greenest island' of his imagination.

England was all bad news for a while: *Hints from Horace* had to give place to what Byron took to be a slighter production of his tour, *Childe Harold's Pilgrimage*; his mother died on August 18 before he got back to Nottinghamshire; while at Newstead he heard of the drowning at Cambridge of his dear friend Charles Skinner Matthews; and, to crown all, in October Byron discovered that his Cambridge favourite, Edlestone, had died in May.

The London of autumn 1811 saw Byron busy with the publication of *Childe Harold* and meeting literary figures like Thomas Moore, and early the following year, in February, Byron made his first speech in the House of Lords. The Bill was the Frame-Breaking Bill and he delivered in a theatrical and artificial manner a speech sarcastic in tone but genuinely in favour of the exploited workers.

Childe Harold's edition was sold out in three days and from that moment onwards Byron was always news in England; fame and notoriety were his for the rest of his life. He became the paradoxical Childe Harold, half-angel, half-devil, and everyone wanted to meet him.

Once in society an affair with the passionate and ill-balanced Lady Caroline Lamb absorbed much of his time, though Annabella Milbanke, Caroline's temperamental opposite, met him on April 14 and he fired Miss Milbanke's ideas of human reclamation. This developed into a slow friendship, and an eventual disastrous marriage on 2 January 1815, but not before other women had come into Byron's life and gone again from it. Lady Caroline caused scandals of magnitude, but eventually he freed himself only to become the final lover of the much-loved Lady Oxford, now in her final flowering and bringing to him material and mistress's comforts. This lasted for eight months; the Oxfords went to Sicily on 29 June 1813 without him, though he had been invited, but he could not raise the money.

Back in London he had a visit from his half-sister and she brought a measure of consolation, maternal and simple, generous and gay, but the outcome was more than either had bargained for. This July stay of Augusta's altered his whole life. The probability is that there was an incestuous relationship, and henceforward Byron's mind was haunted by guilt and secret horror, and a recognition that he was irradicably altered.

Meantime he was publishing his Oriental Tales: *The Giaour* appeared in the spring of 1813, and, just later, *The Corsair* became his best-selling poem to date, having sold ten thousand copies on publication day alone. He was the successful author and the Tales continued to appear until 1816, extremely popular then if almost unread now.

Byron's marriage in January 1815 led to bad behaviour on his part towards his wife, with shows of temper, sarcasm, insults and innuendoes about his love for Augusta and his 'terrible' past. Domestic life in the Byrons' London home was turbulent: creditors heard that he had married an heiress and descended; bailiffs were frequent visitors in the house; Augusta came to stay (probably invited by Annabella); Byron took to late hours and heavy drinking and involved himself in the theatre and theatrical affairs and easy conquests among the actresses. In December the child of the marriage, Augusta Ada, was born, and Byron proposed that mother and daughter retire to her parents' home in Durham. Before they left on January 15 Annabella asked for a medical opinion on Byron, and she now received it: the verdict was that he was sane, though irascible and violent. This was the last straw and he was to become separated from his wife.

London hummed with rumours and he was a living scandal, a social outcast. Ten minutes ahead of the bailiffs he left London on April 23, and sailed from England for the last time on the 25th.

He journeyed to Geneva, pausing particularly at Waterloo, feeling again the excitement of travel, and writing again. En route to Geneva a little after him was another poet and his party, Shelley, Mary Godwin and her step-sister, Claire Clairmont. Claire had managed to become Byron's mistress briefly just before the separation, and now, unknown to him, was pregnant with his child.

The Shelley *ménage* settled itself near to Byron and he established his relations again with Claire. The two poets hugely enjoyed each other's company and spent many hours together until the Shelleys left on August 29 for England.

Canto III of *Childe Harold's Pilgrimage* and *The Prisoner of Chillon* were written in the summer, and in the autumn Byron and Hobhouse left for Milan; then to Verona and, finally, to Venice and its decaying charm. Here dissolute evenings and the daytime study of Armenian absorbed most of his time, though he did find time to complete his drama, *Manfred*, started in Switzerland. He sunk into gloom gradually and he felt that life had no meaning, but he lingered in Venice ill with surfeit until April 17 when he set out for Rome.

He took with him the knowledge that Claire Clairmont had had his child in January, a girl, Clara Allegra, but he remained stubbornly silent to Mary Shelley who had informed him, and he continued to remain so.

Arriving in Rome he was excited by the greatness of the city and all it has meant to western civilisation. This always meant writing to follow, and the fourth canto of *Childe Harold* followed quickly. He returned to Venice and an abundance of women, the 'natives' (as he called them) of the middle and lower classes. The husband of one of his mistresses told him an anecdote once that so appealed to him that it provided the nucleus of a new mock-heroic poem, *Beppo*. A new manner, irreverent, comic and relaxed came to his verse with this poem and drew the public verse much closer to the private prose.

Beppo and Canto IV of *Childe Harold* were published in the spring of 1818, greatly increasing the reputation of the artist-rake, despite the ineffectual anonymity of *Beppo*'s publication. And in the spring too the illegitimate Clara Allegra arrived with the Shelleys for Byron's custody, and she spent most of her short life deposited with various people out of Byron's way.

In the summer Byron was at work on the first canto of *Don Juan*, and this gave his friends various sorts of headaches when it arrived in England with Lord Lauderdale. In a mood of weariness after lengthy discussion and argument about *Don Juan*, in April 1819 he met again the girl he had briefly met a year before as a newly-wed bride, Theresa, Countess Guiccioli. She was now nineteen, married a year to a husband of fifty-eight, and she fell in love with Byron immediately they talked, and Byron himself was ready to settle. The rest of his time in Italy he was intimately connected with Theresa and her family, loving her and talking and plotting rebellion against the Austrians with Pietro Gamba, her brother.

The next years saw Byron continuing *Don Juan* and reflecting his political thinking in his dramas like *Marino Faliero* and *Sardanapalus*. Other interests are reflected in his work *Cain*, thoughts on sin, death and the meaning of life, and his venture with Leigh Hunt, the founding of a literary journal, *The Liberal*. *The Liberal* was short-lived, though it did publish the continuation of Byron's famous satire of this time, *The Vision of Judgment*.

1821 saw the tragic drowning of Shelley off Leghorn and this seriously disturbed Byron. He tried to find relief in the rapid writing of three more cantos of *Don Juan*, but withdrew into a life of routine until his departure for Greece to help the forces of Freedom.

The Greeks hoped for miracles from Byron's coming and he

sailed from Genoa for Leghorn on 15 July 1823, on the first leg of his journey to Greece. The party sailed from Leghorn on 25 July to reach the island of Cephalonia on August 2 with Byron much improved in health and humour. He was back near his beloved Greece and the voyage had done him good. He waited for news from Italy or England but none had arrived until September 1, and he then was uncertain where to land in Greece to do the most good with the money he was provided with, and, because of dissensions among the Greeks on the mainland, he remained until after Christmas, when he sailed for Missolonghi. Here life was unpleasant for others in the cold winter, but Byron was happy and bustling in his organisation of men and materials. He had some kind of seizure on February 15 which left him weak and ill through February and March, but he survived and managed to break a siege of Missolonghi. He had his fatal attack of fever on April 9 which continued despite medical treatment until his death on 19 April 1824.

2

Early Poems

The *Hours of Idleness* was the first collection of his poems which bore his name on the title-page, though there were enough clues in the earlier volumes to give the game away. It had a sale and Byron was thrilled:

> . . . in every Bookseller's I see my *own name*, and *say nothing* but enjoy my *fame* in *secret.*—My last Reviewer, kindly requests me to alter my determination of writing no more.
>
> LETTERS AND JOURNALS I, 142

Harsh treatment and ridicule came to the volume in the October number of *The Satirist,* and its editor, Hewson Clarke, of Emmanuel College, Cambridge, got as good as he gave in the 'Postscript to the Second Edition' and in *English Bards and Scotch Reviewers.*

While Byron was busy with the nucleus of what was to become *English Bards and Scotch Reviewers* in Cambridge and London, the reviews began to warm up:

> If this was one of his Lordship's *school exercises* at Harrow, and he escaped whipping, they have there either an undue respect for lords' bottoms, or they do not deserve the reputation they have acquired.
>
> *Monthly Mirror,* Vol. III (Jan. 1808). Quoted by W. S. Ward, 'Byron's *Hours of Idleness* and other than Scotch Reviewers', MLN, Vol. LIX (June, 1944)

One of the striking things for a reader nowadays is to notice the ways (and there are many) in which Byron is an 18th-century poet. Of course his poems are derivative, and other poets' voices are heard through Byron's verse, but it is interesting to notice who they are. In many cases this is easy. The critic of the

Edinburgh Review (whose famous attack started with 'The poesy of this young lord belongs to the class which neither gods nor men are said to permit. Indeed, we do not recollect to have seen a quantity of verse with so few deviations in either direction from that exact standard') treats his readers to a derogatory comparison of Gray's *Ode on a Distant Prospect of Eton College* with Byron's *On a Distant View of the Village and School of Harrow*, and of 'the exquisite lines of Mr. Rogers, *On a Tear*' with Byron's similar poem.

Byron indulges in a conventional melancholy and doesn't have Gray's real emotions to give any power to his poem, and he was obviously inviting comparison of his poem with Gray's. The verdict was bound to be against him. He mimics Rogers's sentimentality, but doesn't have even Rogers's fluidity and experience in handling words as musically interesting. Byron is self-indulgent and posturing as a pseudo-Gray; he's almost a limerick writer in *The Tear*:

> Too oft is a smile but the hypocrite's wile,
> > To mask detestation or fear;
> Give me the soft sigh, while the soul-telling eye
> > Is dimm'd for a time with a Tear.

But Byron ranges all over the previous century. His lines, *To the Duke of Dorset*, for example, give us the couplet:

> Then share with titled crowds the common lot—
> In life just gazed at, in the grave forgot;

which is simply an echo of Pope's:

> A fop their passion, but their prize a sot,
> Alive ridiculous, and dead, forgot!

MORAL ESSAYS, Epistle II, 247–8

This reflection of Pope's manner here is only one indication among many of Byron's continuing reverence and love of Pope throughout his life. He championed him against the fashionable society poet, Bowles, and while at Cambridge he annotated his own copy of Owen Ruffhead's *The Life of Alexander Pope*.

In the same poem Byron tries out another Augustan satiric trick, the catalogue:

> There sleep, unnoticed as the gloomy vaults
> That veil their dust, their follies, and their faults.

Here there is no bite, no subtlety as one would find it in Swift or Pope. We might remember *The Rape of the Lock*:

> Puffs, powders, patches, Bibles, billets-doux.

and see what could be done with a succession of items.

The *Elegy on Newstead Abbey* gives us the mid-century style of Dr. Johnson's *The Vanity of Human Wishes*, and, though Byron's poem is written in stanzas and not in heroic couplets, there is something of the quality of Johnson's handling of verse and a note of the dark inevitability of fate.

> Years roll on years; to ages, ages yield;
> Abbots to abbots, in a line, succeed;
> Religion's charter their protecting shield,
> Till royal sacrilege their doom decreed.[1]

Dr. Johnson's lines obviously reverberated in Byron's mind because he used echoes from the same poem again in *To a Youthful Friend*, 1808:

> Such is the common lot of man:
> Can we then 'scape from folly free?
> Can we reverse the general plan,
> Nor be what all in turn must be?[2]

Of course, one sees that Byron is manipulating stage properties, even some that are a little rusty with disuse. The theatrical

---

[1] Year chases year, decay pursues decay,
Still drops some joy from with'ring life away;
New forms arise, and diff'rent views engage,
Superfluous lags the vet'ran on the stage,
Till pitying Nature signs the last release,
And bids afflicted worth retire to peace.

THE VANITY OF HUMAN WISHES, 305–10

[2] Yet hope not life from grief or danger free,
Nor think the doom of man reversed for thee.

IBID. 115–6

gesturing can be seen, along with some of the 'effects' of the sentimental graveyard school of writing, in

> Within this narrow cell reclines her clay,
>> That clay, where once such animation beam'd;
> The King of Terrors seized her as his prey,
>> Not worth nor beauty have her life redeem'd.

ON THE DEATH OF A YOUNG LADY, 1802

Out of much that is execrable one might notice the cliché,
narrow cell for *grave*; the abstraction for the concrete, *animation
beam'd*, and I can't imagine anything much slacker than that.
Even the hidden metaphor in *beam'd*, which Pope makes such
excellent use of in *The Rape of the Lock*, is left to lie peacefully.
It must be said to Byron's credit, perhaps, that he did use the
metaphor somewhat as a mocking joke in *To Edward Long, Esq.*

> And Cora's eye, which roll'd on me,
>> Can now no more my love recall:
> In truth, dear LONG, 'twas time to flee;
>> For Cora's eye will shine on all.

> And though the sun, with genial rays,
> His beams alike to all displays,
> And every lady's eye's a *sun*,
> These last should be confin'd to one.
> The soul's meridian don't become her,
> Whose sun displays a general *summer!*

Byron takes the poeticism of eyes and suns and enjoys a joke
at the expense both of himself and the faithless girl. Pope's use
is both wittier and wiser, more delicate, excluding deliberately
any suggestion of sexual promiscuity, working by suggestion
and implication, the nuance, the glance:

> Her lively looks a sprightly mind disclose,
> Quick as her eyes, and as unfix'd as those:
> Favours to none, to all she smiles extends;
> Oft she rejects, but never once offends.
> Bright as the sun, her eyes the gazers strike,
> And, like the sun, they shine on all alike.

THE RAPE OF THE LOCK, Canto II, 10–14

24

Byron is jauntier, more conversational, and certainly more impressed with his own joke. He demands a guffaw from his friend rather than the cooler response, more complex in itself, demanded by Pope.

Much of the reader's response to the *Hours of Idleness* is like this, sometimes appalled by the solemnity with which the trite is offered as the serious, and sometimes joyed at finding the mocking ability to stand aside and witness the falseness of it all. We move, say, from *The Tear*'s absurdity, awash with all the sentimental tears of this unfortunate literary vogue of the later 18th century, to *To Romance*. Here we have an interesting reflection on Byron's own verse and that of the fashionable contemporary mode of light verse. It points to the sort of poetry Byron was increasingly capable of—a harder-edged, less vaguely emotional verse. It points to that hard-headedness which commentators on Byron have been fond of noticing (the fact that he could later become careful—canny—over money, for example). It points too to the sober empiricism of the English philosophy which dominated the 18th century, the reliance on what can be apprehended by the senses, the mind as a block of wax 'impressed' with 'ideas' coming to it from without. We can see Byron as able to see his own stance and that of his literary manner as unreal and playful rather than as serious and realistic. When he says:

> No more I tread thy mystic round,
>   But leave thy realms for those of Truth

we might think of Keats and his recognition of the need to leave Sleep and Fancy for 'Truth', but we would have to recognise that Keats's Truth would be that of the Imagination and Vision. Byron's Truth would be rather a synonym for Fact, a more modern conception. It is this sort of modernity which the critics tend to see in the later poems, but we might do well to recognise it here too:

> Romance! disgusted with deceit,
>   Far from thy motley court I fly,
> Where Affection holds her seat,
>   And sickly Sensibility;

Whose silly tears can never flow
   For any pangs excepting thine;
Who turns aside from real woe,
   To steep in dew thy gaudy shrine.

Now join with sable *Sympathy*,
   With cypress crown'd, array'd in weeds,
Who heaves with thee her simple sigh,
   Whose breast for every bosom bleeds;
And call thy sylvan female choir,
   To mourn a swain for ever gone,
Who once could glow with equal fire,
   But bends not now before thy throne.

One might say that it seems quite obvious that Byron is simply rejecting that false way of celebrating emotions under the flag of 'Sensibility' which vitiates much of the later 18th-century writing, of which the best example might be Sterne's *A Sentimental Journey*. Yet there the matter does not end at all. Byron retains enough of what he himself later pilloried as 'sensibilitous' to make one feel that he is still tied to this way of exciting emotions for their own sake and of wallowing in the sensitive response to an imagined situation. In this collection of poems the lament stands out as sentimental in just those ways that Byron himself condemns in his poem on *Romance*. The paraphrase of *The Episode of Nisus and Euryalus*, a moment of elegiac lament for the death of the beautiful youth, is sugared, chintzy and artificial:

Lowly to earth inclines his plume-clad crest,
And sanguine torrents mantle o'er his breast:
As some young rose, whose blossom scents the air,
Languid in death, expires beneath the share;
Or crimson poppy, sinking with the shower,
Declining gently, falls a fading flower;
Thus, sweetly drooping, bends his lovely head,
And lingering beauty hovers round his head.

We have so much of the vulgar Byron here that it is worth recording for that only: the 'artistry' (the over-conscious alliteration of 'falls a fading flower'), the sentiment hot-house and yet distant, the parade, the slackness of artistic hold. In another context Byron attempted to make a distinction between vulgarity and coarseness; I think that here he falls within his own condemnation:

> The grand distinction of the under forms of the new school of poets is their *vulgarity*. By this I do not mean that they are *coarse*, but 'shabby-genteel', as it is termed. A man may be *coarse* and yet not *vulgar*, and the reverse. Burns is often coarse, but never *vulgar*. Chatterton is never vulgar, nor Wordsworth, nor the higher of the Lake school, though they treat of low life in all its branches. It is in their *finery* that the new under school are *most* vulgar, and they may be known by this at once; as what we called at Harrow 'a Sunday blood' might be easily distinguished from a gentleman, although his clothes might be the better cut, and his boots the best blackened, of the two;—probably because he made the one, or cleaned the other, with his own hands.

> A Second Letter on Bowles's Strictures on the Life and Writings of Pope, THE WORKS OF LORD BYRON, by Thomas Moore, Vol. VI 413–14

Later Byron distrusted expression of emotion, though he remained capable of sentimentality, and he needed constantly to reduce sentiment to mockery or to counter it by an emetic. But even these tactics would seem to indicate someone in whom sentimentality was rooted.

One more noteworthy thing about the lament poems, again on the debit side, is that of Byron's ear and its insensitivity. This can show itself in simple ways which are all the more striking. We notice, for example, the mechanical caesurae, as in

> Veil'd by the night,/secure the Trojan lies.
> Burning with wrath,/he view'd his soldiers fall,
> 'Thou youth accurst,/thy life shall pay for all!'
> THE EPISODE OF NISUS AND EURYALUS 358–60

Or we are struck (for the worse) by his choice of rhythm. He seems to have set his teeth determinedly for a cheerful rhythm, despite his topic and the supposed mood. *On Leaving Newstead*

Abbey shows an experiment with metrics, and the lament poem, obviously an occasion for sentimental outpourings (one would imagine), here contrives to gallop along in the anapaestic rhythm most of us associate with the heavily anthologised *The Assyrian came down like the wolf on the fold.* He prefixes his poem with a piece from the fashionable *Ossian,* the apparently genuine Celtic poetry which had stirred the imagination of cultural Europe during the later 18th century. As the author, James Macpherson, claimed, his poems

> must be confessed, are more calculated to please persons of exquisite feelings of heart, than those who receive all their impressions by the ear.
>
> Preface to THE POEMS OF OSSIAN, London, 1805

This sentimental mode conflicts with the basic cheerfulness of the rhythm in Byron's poem with a result that is almost comic:

> Through thy battlements, Newstead, the hollow winds whistle;
>   Thou, the hall of my fathers, art gone to decay;
> In thy once smiling garden, the hemlock and thistle
>   Have choked up the rose which late bloom'd in the way.

It may be granted that parts of this poem do prance in a martial way, but other poems in the same rhythm come nowhere near the martial. Everything pays homage to this tyrant of an anapaestic throb; thought, emotion, sincerity:

> Now hate rules a heart in love's easy chains
>   Once passion's tumultuous blandishments knew;
> Despair now inflames the dark tide of his veins;
>   He ponders in frenzy on love's last adieu!
>
> LOVE'S LAST ADIEU 25–8

No one could believe the 'frenzy' here, and the theatricality and hollowness of the language is too nearly funny for anyone to take seriously the poet's blighted heart. Still, one might say that the sprightliness of the rhythm belongs to an attempt, alas only too unsuccessful, to escape some of the current sentimentality.

It is this sprightliness and jauntiness which keeps coming through the writing, taking the form of self-mockery, joking or extempore writing in the style of a Sterne or a Fielding. The satire on Cambridge, *Granta*, 1806, though tame enough as satire, does indicate something of the ease with which Byron could manage both colloquial tone and artistic form, a mechanism both for self-display and for the reduction of solemnity of thought. This, of course, will figure most largely in his final poems. In this poem the irreverence and comedy of the singing choir is a faint sign of what he can do in the later *The Vision of Judgment* (perhaps one ought to say very faint):

> If David, when his toils were ended,
>> Had heard these blockheads sing before him,
> To use his Psalms had ne'er descended,—
>> In furious mood he would have tore 'em.

The rhyme 'before him'/'tore 'em' is adolescent impishness, but the habit of mockery, whether at solemn notions, solemn verse or solemn expression, is part of Byron's armoury, and it is good to note it here at the start of his career.

In this piece too we have the reflection on the *process* of writing as it is being written, rather than the attitude of studious care in presenting the product, again one of Byron's strengths and habits of mind.

> But if I scribble longer now,
>> The deuce a soul will stay to read;
> My pen is blunt, my ink is low;
>> 'Tis almost time to stop, indeed.

This gives the cachet of the rather carefree, careless writer who enjoys his writing, doesn't see it as a task or primary occupation, but something for which he has a happy knack, a facility. Byron always wanted to give the lie to the idea that he was a *writer*, disassociating himself from professional writers in his own mind, though a real craftsman himself. We have to wait a good while until we can relish the success of this carefree manner properly, until we can read poetry like this manuscript stanza written on the MS of *Don Juan* in 1818:

I would to heaven that I were so much clay,
    As I am blood, bone, marrow, passion, feeling—
Because at least the past were pass'd away—
    And for the future—(but I write this reeling,
Having got drunk exceedingly today,
    So that I seem to stand upon the ceiling)
I say—the future is a serious matter—
And so—for God's sake—hock and soda-water!

Though the use of satire connects Byron quite firmly with the
preceding century and its major literary form, there is a poem
written about this time, but unpublished until after Byron's
death, which deserves mention here. *The Prayer of Nature* tells
us several important things about Byron and the 18th century.
As a whole the poem echoes Pope's *The Universal Prayer*, and
Byron tries to maintain a similar theological position of ignoring
sects and formal religion, though believing in a First Mover and
Controller, but having no notion of a personal God:

Shall man confine his Maker's sway
    To Gothic domes of mouldering stone?
Thy temple is the face of day;
    Earth, ocean, heaven, thy boundless throne.

Side by side with this we have the echo of Swift's hatred of the
petty warring religious sects, the anger at the lack of common
sense and man's foolish pride in his own ideas of God, necessarily limited and therefore wrong. In Swift's poem *The Day of
Judgment*, written in 1731, he reached a pitch of savagery, imagin-
ing God (Jove) watching all men coming up for judgment:

The world's mad business now is o'er,
And I resent these pranks no more.
—I to such blockheads set my wit!
I damn such fools!—Go, go, you're bit.

The dark rage of the poem doesn't permit the reader to appraise
Swift's position, but he is made to in Byron's poem. There is
much personal uncertainty, more anguish at the unknown:

I own myself corrupt and weak,
    Yet will I pray for thou wilt hear!

The reader cannot be certain about the force of '*wilt* hear' for he feels that there is an undermining uncertainty of faith in the poem. The conditional 'if——then' clauses which frame the thinking about the soul and its immortality in the last three stanzas do not carry, by their nature, that soaring *credo* which one might look for in a hymn. The poem ends with a hope, not a conviction:

> To Thee I breathe my humble strain,
> > Grateful for all thy mercies past,
> And hope, my God, to thee again
> > This erring life may fly at last.

A poem written the following year, *The Adieu*, sums up the theme of the Hymn in a final stanza, though this time the prayer is not even one of hope, but a downward-moving prayer for instruction in dying:

> And, since I soon must cease to live,
> > Instruct me how to die.

This leaden quality also rhymes with the obvious predestinarian basis of Byron's thinking, and this is the source of much of the anxiety in the poem:

> Can vice atone for crimes by prayer?
>
> Shall those, who live for self alone,
> > Whose years float on in daily crime—
> Shall they by Faith for guilt atone,
> > And live beyond the bounds of Time?

Though Byron was often thought shocking by some of his contemporaries, there is the important residual truth that, at heart, he was convinced of damnation, of the fallen condition of man. A modern critic, trying to schematise the Romantic poets, draws a distinction between Christian and non-Christian, with Blake, Byron and Coleridge as 'Christian', and Wordsworth, Keats and Shelley as 'non-Christian'. He says that Byron

> who shared Blake's and Shelley's liberalism, never allowed that bias to deflect for one moment his conviction of the ineradicable human

taint. From this point of view he is the most 'orthodox' of the Romantics.

Bernard Blackstone, THE LOST TRAVELLERS, 1962, p. 10

Finally the love poems deserve a line or so. Byron was very pleased indeed with having given the impression of being a most profligate sinner, and, though I'm not willing to argue what constitutes profligacy and how far Byron qualifies, I would be willing to say that his verse is by Thomas Moore out of Samuel Rogers. Writing to his young friend, John M. B. Pigot, he tells him that

> That *unlucky* poem to my poor Mary has been the cause of some animadversion from *Ladies in years*. I have not printed it in the collection, in consequence of my being pronounced a most *profligate sinner*, in short, a 'young Moore', by ——, your friend. I believe, in general, they have been favourably received, and surely the age of their author will preclude severe criticism. The adventures of my life from sixteen to nineteen, and the dissipation into which I have been thrown in London, have given a voluptuous tint to my ideas; but the occasions which called forth my muse could hardly admit any other colouring. This volume is *vastly* correct and miraculously chaste.
>
> LETTERS AND JOURNALS I, 112–13. 13 January 1807

Again the claim to being 'truthful', something which will be noted so constantly as to become a hallmark of the best of Byron's writing.

To sum up the qualities of Byron's first acknowledged volume, *Hours of Idleness*, we might say that the verse is very humdrum and derivative on the whole, using some of the strengths of 18th-century writing. It is sentimental and posturing, but with some indications of a bent towards the more colloquial, more realistic expression of a non-Romantic outlook; an overall failure of the ear to organise sound in a musical way, mechanical rhythms in formal metres, but a good ear for the spoken phrase and manner.

3

'English Bards and Scotch Reviewers'

In reply to what Byron took to be the over-savage slashing of a youthful poem by the *Edinburgh Review*, he took up that attitude which demands maturity, that of the surgeon-writer who wrote 'if possible, to make others write better'. He was going to show that he was a brave man who would neither be frightened nor silenced, and one who could tell the scribblers something about their real worth, an indictment of the debasers of the art of letters, engaging in 'mental prostitution'; 'perverted powers demand the most decided reprehension'. In short, a new *Dunciad*.

Though he attacks energetically and with physical power:

> Prepare for rhyme—I'll publish, right or wrong:
> Fools are my theme, let satire be my song.

there would seem to be several difficulties in the method of treatment he had adopted. Pope's *Dunciad* has a structure which can be seen at least partially to depend on a plot, a set of narrative events, and has an epic structure (even if mock-epic). Byron has only a catalogue of enemies, major and minor, and a few hero-figures, but the enemies only exist to be knocked down and have no apparent life within the poem. Perhaps more importantly, he has only the skin and bones of Pope's technique, with none of that inner personal handling of the heroic couplet which is the reflection of a habit of mind, a culture, and a carefully-held decorum. What is apparent in Byron's poem is that he has to keep the personal for a digression outside the frame, unlike Pope whose couplets in their manipulation are simultaneously an expression of the personal and of the public and ethical. But it is Byron's easy manner of being autobiographical and digressive which might impress the reader, for good or ill, when one might have expected the author to be getting on with things. It is this quality, the digressive, easy wandering, which will become something to intrigue in *Childe Harold's Pilgrimage* and something to relish in the last satires, *Beppo* and *Don Juan*.

After the usual review of the relation of satire to vice and folly, and admitting that 'the royal vices of our age' need a better hand than his own, Byron views the quarry, the 'scribblers':

> ye strains of great and small,
> Ode, epic, elegy, have at you all!

and one might expect him to give chase. But no. He then, almost conversationally, talks of himself:

> I too can scrawl, and once upon a time
> I pour'd along the town a flood of rhyme,
> A schoolboy freak, unworthy praise or blame;
> I printed—older children do the same.
> 'Tis pleasant, sure, to see one's name in print;
> A book's a book, although there's nothing in 't.

47-52

This sort of passage rivets one's attention on the speaker, and one is meant to be disarmed or charmed by the revelations and by the apparent sophistication of the attitude of the speaker to himself and to us. The public voice of the outraged Augustan satirist using a public-address system here changes to that of a man with attitudes, able to assume or drop the public voice, the public gesture, the public flogging of the satiric object, for the private musing or quiet confidence.

It is this anomalous duality of tone which certainly strikes the reader, the coexistence of a modern and an ancient voice. After a passage of dialogue on the relation of Byron's satire to that of earlier satirists like Pope and Gifford (whose *Baviad* and *Maeviad* were imitations of the *Dunciad*), Byron starts to speak like Pope or a more 18th-century Dryden, using standard critical terms of the 18th century like 'degenerate days', 'sense', 'wit', 'taste', and 'reason', and adopting an older voice and manner. This is almost a voice from the past telling about modern degeneration from these criteria, and is certainly not Byron's voice at all:

> Time was, ere yet in these degenerate days
> Ignoble themes obtain'd mistaken praise,
> When sense and wit with poesy allied,
> No fabled graces, flourish'd side by side;
> From the same fount their inspiration drew,
> And, rear'd by taste, bloom'd fairer as they grew.
>
> 103–8

Against both the ceremony of these lines and their classical substructure we have to set the new literature:

> The cow-pox, tractors, galvanism, and gas,
> In turns appear, to make the vulgar stare,
> Till the swoln bubble bursts—and all is air!
>
> 132–4

Though one might share Byron's feelings, the verse is certainly entirely lacking in punch and destructive force; no wit, no bite.

Byron then as Inspector-General inspects the current vogues in literature, passing in review each as it occurs to him, and spending some time and rhetoric in admonishing what he sees to be puerile. So the *Lay of the Last Minstrel* gets scolded:

> While high-born ladies in their magic cell,
> Forbidding knights to read who cannot spell,
> Despatch a courier to a wizard's grave,
> And fight with honest men to shield a knave.
>
> 161–4

Scott collects more bad marks for Marmion's 'stale romance', and for the author's being one of those 'Who rack their brains for lucre, not for fame', while Southey, seen in the context of the great epic poets, is very uncivilly treated. Byron treats him as a joke, and so can joke on him:

> But if, in spite of all the world can say,
> Thou still wilt verseward plod thy weary way . . .
> 'God help thee,' Southey, and thy readers too.
>
> 229–30, 234

Byron's note to this passage continues the joke by not reminding the reader of Gray's ploughman, but by directing him rather to a plagiarism of the more contemporary political journal, *Anti-Jacobin*:

> The last line, 'God help thee,' is an evident plagiarism from the Anti-Jacobin to Mr. Southey, on his Dactylics.

Byron goes through the writers in literary vogue one by one and has a smack, more or less violent, at each one. He gives, interestingly perhaps, one of the lightest taps to Thomas Moore. Moore was to become Byron's friend and first biographer; he was then the

> young Catullus of his day,
> As sweet, but as immoral, in his lay!

287-8

Now he is 'Irish Melodies' Moore and harmless enough, but Byron in his role as moral arbiter ought to have knocked him down severely for his 'immoral lay'. Apparently all that the Muse demands in his case is an expiation and all will be well; no severity there, one would think.

A poet who is linked with Moore (under his pseudonymn of 'Little') is Bowles; his verse is seen as appealing to 'the mania of the amorous throng' in the same sense as Moore's. But Byron takes exception to his verse and not to Moore's. Officially it is because Bowles is 'The maudlin prince of mournful sonneteers', a sixty-year-old man who writes under the heading of Sympathy, that superheated and false emotional code of the end of the previous century. One really feels that Bowles offers sentimentality to *young* girls, but that Little is stronger meat for the more mature:

> With thee our nursery damsels shed their tears,
> Ere miss as yet completes her infant years:
> But in her teens thy whining powers are vain;
> She quits poor Bowles for Little's purer strain.

345-8

But the real reason for the antipathy is rather because Bowles had attacked the character of Pope, one of Byron's master poets, and Byron is taking revenge.

The trouble is that Byron is not fitted either by temperament or experience for the role of superintendent of literary morals or proprieties. He's quite capable of gibing in a rather schoolboy manner, as when he introduces Amos Cottle, the Bristol merchant-poet, and blurts out:

> Oh, Amos Cottle!—Phoebus! what a name
> To fill the speaking trump of future fame!—
>
> 399–400

This sort of one-upmanship, an ungentlemanly act we might think, is just what Byron takes to be his gentlemanly prerogative, and he can do this sort of thing side by side with his attempt to be like Pope in the *Dunciad* creating an almost surrealist absurdity. The minor poet, Maurice, for example, is seen as a sort of Sisyphus rolling his stone everlastingly uphill:

> As Sisyphus against the infernal steep
> Rolls the huge rock whose motions ne'er may sleep,
> So up thy hill, ambrosial Richmond, heaves
> Dull Maurice all his granite weight of leaves:
> Smooth, solid monuments of mental pain!
> The petrifactions of a plodding brain,
> That, ere they reach the top, fall lumbering back again.
>
> 411–17

Of course, this does not come off like Pope's creations, precisely because the whole thing is too mechanical and one does not see the wit or the absurdity as one would do in Pope. Byron simply uses the myth of Sisyphus without really making it come alive for us in a new way.

After having some fun with the rather humdrum joke about the critic Jeffrey's name being similar to the infamous hanging Judge Jeffries, and of their equal inhumanity and injustice, he has even more fun with the duel between Thomas Moore and Jeffrey. Though Byron's target was Jeffrey rather than Moore, Byron perpetuates a standing joke about the duel where it was found that only one of the pair of pistols that Moore presented was loaded. Jeffrey gets treated to something like the coarseness and vileness which Pope builds into the *Dunciad*, which one is forced to excuse by invoking 'the rough manners of the age', I suppose.

His treatment of contemporary theatre, what there was, is fairly feeble, probably because he feels, rightly, that there's nothing much to lash; he does shine a little more brightly in his treatment of the foreign opera and ballet. His objection to these is two-fold: they encourage licentiousness by the display of the human person in far too immodest dress on stage; and they are a living example of English hypocrisy. To keep the Sabbath holy no beer can be sold on Sundays, and no barber can shave his customers, and yet we are allowed by the law to have these immodest displays. Byron is not simple in his attitude here; he is both puritan and libertarian, one might say, though he remained a good hater of English hypocrisy throughout his life. Similarly, he frowns on assemblies where the 'loose waltz' is danced, where female display is a sort of prostitution, and most distasteful to Byron both in his public role and in his personal life:

> Those for Hibernia's lusty sons repair
> With art the charms which nature could not spare;
> These after husbands wing their eager flight
> Nor leave much mystery for the nuptial night.

664-7

Byron was to devote a whole satire four years later to the 'not too lawfully begotten "Waltz"'. This *Apostrophic Hymn* is a more extended puritanical outburst against what Byron saw as the sexual licence of the dance, outraging decency, and poisoning love and sex by a cheap display and public contact. A shout and a sneer, but enlivened by the occasional bite, as in:

> To you, ye single gentlemen, who seek
> Torments for life, or pleasures for a week,
> As Love or Hymen your endeavours guide,
> To gain your own, or snatch another's bride:—

103-6

In this later poem, as here, we do find a wit which is more Augustan than in the earlier satire. This peculiarly witty *double entendre* works simply but effectively: one can see Love lasting for a week and Hymen for life, but Love might give a life of torments (if one contracts venereal disease) and Hymen might give a week's pleasures (with a life of torments in a nagging wife).

However, in *English Bards and Scotch Reviewers* Byron sees the Waltz as only one of the evils encouraged by the houses of the great, the 'blest retreats of infamy and ease', and he has a long digression only loosely attached, one might think, to his central topic. Within this long digression he has a further where he does some self-examination. Instead of the anonymous satirist's voice, the sane voice among lunatics, Byron's is only one among those of the lunatics. But, he says, even he must raise his voice because

> Such scenes, such men, destroy the public weal:

He says that the sight of *Byron* protesting may seem odd, but there it is:

> And every brother rake will smile to see
> That miracle, a moralist in me.

699–700

The personal voice, individual and smilingly serious, is certainly Byron's and the pose of the rake is habitual and perhaps deserved, but both these facts make the sound of the verse unAugustan.

After bestowing words of praise on those poets whom he finds congenial and honest, Byron takes his leave. It is curious that of the contemporary poets whom Byron backs here, all but one are losers; of Gifford, Sotheby, Macneil, White, Crabbe and Shee only Crabbe remains of real permanent interest. But they are, for Byron, honest ('Feel as they write, and write but as they feel') or, like Crabbe, are truthful:

> Yet Truth sometimes will lend her noblest fires,
> And decorate the verse herself inspires:

39

This fact in Virtue's name let Crabbe attest;
Though nature's sternest painter, yet the best.

855-8

Being Byron he is very conscious that his personal verbal attacks might provoke physical attacks; these he welcomes and utters a general challenge, as a good man of honour, proud of his name and courage, should. It's bravado, but it's Byron:

And though I hope not hence unscathed to go,
Who conquers me shall find a stubborn foe.

1051-2

And in the *Postscript to the Second Edition* he returns to this duelling motif:

It may be said that I quit England because I have censured there 'persons of honour and wit about town'; but I am coming back again, and their vengeance will keep hot till my return. . . . Since the publication of this thing, my name has not been concealed; I have been mostly in London, ready to answer for my transgressions, and in daily expectation of sundry cartels; but, alas! 'the age of chivalry is over', or, in the vulgar tongue, there is no spirit now-a-days.

So Byron took his revenge for the treatment of his first volume of poetry, but his medium was uncomfortable and he did little service to the cause of the Augustan satire; but he did point to some of those qualities of ease and digression in an almost unbuttoned manner which were to be his own answer to native inability to write well in restricted form. Some wit, but not enough; some spirit, but more perhaps in the footnotes; some originality but much more of commonplace thoughts in conventional and anonymous expression. We must judge the poem now on whatever merits we can discover, but in the early 19th century it was possible to be so in love with Byron that this poem was accepted simply as Satire. Or at least one might gather this from an anonymous satire, *The Dunciad of Today*, published in a short-lived periodical called *The Star Chamber* in 1826. Benjamin Disraeli is thought to have written it, though the evidence for this is only indirect, and he certainly shows a great admiration for Byron's work. The satire opens by quoting Byron's satire and continues with much praise and adulation.

> 'Fools are my theme!'—indignant Byron cried,
> And vengeful Satire back'd the poet's pride.
>
> Quench'd is that spirit now; long toss'd and torn,
> At home distracted, and abroad forlorn,
> Caprice and frenzy rack'd his feverish brain,
> Till soothing Fancy shed her dews in vain. . . . etc. etc.
>
> Benjamin Disraeli, THE DUNCIAD OF TODAY AND THE MODERN AESOP

Byron becomes Disraeli's model for the writing of an even more modern *Dunciad* than Byron's; but both are minor works.

4

'Childe Harold's Pilgrimage' I & II

Of the two major productions of Byron's tour of 1809–1811 Byron backed the satiric work, *Hints from Horace*. This was largely a literal verse translation of Horace's *Ars Poetica*, the loose notes of the Latin satirist on writing, known officially as *Ad Pisones, De Arte Poetica*. In the title Byron says that it is 'Intended as a Sequel to "English Bards and Scotch Reviewers"'.

It is sad to say that this work is unmusical and largely dull, with only occasional acerbities; it is far too closely tied to Horace and, though sometimes clever in finding modern parallels for Horatian persons and situations, most of the good things fritter themselves away in rather ponderous succeeding lines:

> Then glide down Grub-street—fasting and forgot;
> Laugh'd into Lethe by some quaint Review,
> Whose wit is never troublesome till—true.

34–6

The parade of alliteration only seems to succeed in the succinctness of 'fasting and forgot', but this clashes with 'glide down Grub-street', a set of four words unequally weighed and unequally related, and the line fails to fulfil itself in the labour of the following couplet.

His own motto seems quite enough, and one wonders if he could take his own and Horace's advice:

> Sometimes a sprightly wit, and tale well told,
> Without much grace, or weight, or art, will hold
> A longer empire o'er the public mind
> Than sounding trifles, empty, though refined.

505–8

There is only an occasional felicity of phrase, showing the 'sprightly wit', and having something of the immediacy of the speaking voice that the most congenial verse of Byron's has:

> Dogs blink their covey, flints withhold the spark,
> And double-barrels (damn them!) miss their mark.

555–6

This excellent touch makes both lighter and more modern and personal Horace's much simpler line:

> *Nec semper feriet quodcunque minabitur arcus.*

But Byron is not simply translating Horace; he is able from time to time to interpolate passages of his own like ll. 689–96, a reflection on the Muse by way of an attack on the hypocrisy of women. The obvious parallel for the passage is Pope's Narcissa, and it goes without saying that Pope makes a much more savage job than does Byron. Pope's antithetical balance in his lines and in his thought gives a picture not simply of a social or sexual hypocrite, but of a complex person with antagonistic motivations. Byron's portrait is slacker, more mechanical and imitative:

> The Muse, like mortal females, may be woo'd;
> In turn she'll seem a Paphian, or a prude;
> Fierce as a bride when first she feels affright,
> Mild as the same upon the second night;
> Wild as the wife of alderman or peer,
> Now for his grace, and now a grenadier!
> Her eyes beseem, her heart belies, her zone,
> Ice in a crowd, and lava when alone.

689–96

Once again, Byron has chosen the wrong medium for his own poetic gifts, and heroic couplets lead him into bad Popean imitation and pastiche; but we ought to remember that he had little choice for a public vehicle of communication when his purpose was satire of this formal sort. It was unfortunate that he thought that this sort of satire was his metier; it was not, as the later satires were to show.

Meantime, Byron had a completely different sort of poem, less public, which he thought less of initially, and yet this was the work which jumped him into both instant fame and public worship. This was *Childe Harold's Pilgrimage, A Romaunt*. Here Byron turned from the heroic couplet to the Spenserian stanza, a nine-line stanza of five-stress lines ending with one with six stresses, and rhyming in three linked sounds, ababbcbcc. It had been popular through the 18th century and in his *Preface* Byron quotes Beattie and Thomson as practitioners. One of the reasons Byron quotes Beattie is that Beattie discovered the stanza as admitting of 'every variety', something that ought to have suited Byron's *mobilité*, his rapid shuttling from mood to mood, making his writing able to grow nearer and nearer to real life and real experiences. Beattie says:

> Not long ago, I began a poem in the style and stanza of Spenser, in which I propose to give full scope to my inclination, and be either droll or pathetic, descriptive or sentimental, tender or satirical, as the humour strikes me; for, if I mistake not, the measure which I have adopted admits equally of all these kinds of composition.

This certainly attracted Byron, and though the poem recreates Byron's own tour it is not simply a travelogue but does approach nearer to actual experience. Unfortunately, Byron is still an amateur really and falls into several traps. One of these is the stanza itself. It is made famous in *The Faerie Queene* and Byron cannot avoid Spenserianisms and archaisms, despite the fact that the poem's situation, protagonists and experiences are contemporary. The archaisms merely annoy and get in the way; but one notices that they are thickest at the start of the poem and as it progresses they get fewer and fewer.

It is important to remember that Byron's poem falls into the fag-end of the tradition of topographical poetry in England. This was a long and honourable tradition which had been seen as a poetry

> . . . throughout which, the descriptions of places, and images raised by the poet, are still tending to some hint, or leading into

some reflection, upon moral life, or political institutions; much in the same manner as the real sight of such scenes and prospects is apt to give the mind a composed turn, and incline it to thoughts and contemplations that have a relation to the object . . .

So wrote Joseph Warton in his *Essays on the Genius and Writings of Pope* (4th ed. 1782, I, 31), and we can take this as a representative statement about the literary kind and see that the person versed in the tradition would take easily to Byron's poem. Though we might take Warton's statement as representing the standard 18th-century view of this sort of poetry, a modern reader is rather anxious about Byron's Childe. How far is he to be identified with Byron? Childe Harold is dissociated by the author from himself in the poem, but he can be seen to be the first of a long list of what have become familiar Byronic heroes, damned, satiated and suffering from hopeless love. This one has run 'through Sin's long labyrinth' and

> With pleasure drugg'd, he almost long'd for woe,
> And e'en for change of scene would seek the shades below.
>
> I, *vi*

He is a melodramatic and sketchy figure into whom Byron siphoned part of his own malaise, his own feelings and responses when in a particular mood. It must be remembered that Byron only represents part of his complex personality here, but it truly was a part. Byron's problem was not simply to convince the reader that he was not to be identified with Harold, but it was to run two characters in harness in a non-dramatic poem. It is often very difficult and perhaps not profitable to decide who thinks what in the poem; Byron quickly tires of the attempt to keep the Childe in his own or the reader's mind, and he drops him progressively through the poem.

What Byron wants to do is to write a poem which will use all his experience, reflections and meditations on his journey and to link these by introducing a 'fictitious character' who will give 'some connexion to the piece'. But his attitude to his hero is fluid, offering him as interesting, a new sort of Gothic hero, and also as someone rather silly, or at least incredible.

He is equally unhappy about this form of stanza and he hardly knows what to do with the final alexandrine, the line of twelve syllables that supplies the cadence to each stanza; and he does not seem very clear about the real poetic possibilities of the stanza. He uses the alexandrine as a simple tag line, for example, in a stanza of impressionistic leaping from detail to detail of Cintra:

> The horrid crags, by toppling convent crown'd,
> The cork-trees hoar that clothe the craggy steep,
> The mountain-moss by scorching skies imbrown'd
> The sunken glen, whose sunless shrubs must weep,
> The tender azure of the unruffled deep,
> The orange tints that gild the greenest bough,
> The torrents that from cliff to valley leap,
> The vine on high, the willow branch below,
> Mix'd in one mighty scene, with varied beauty glow.

> I, *xix*

There seems no reason why the catalogue should end, and certainly no reason why the final line should be so exhausted and flat. Because, despite the conventional 18th-century words ('horrid', 'imbrown'd'), there is a freshness of vision, a real continuation of experience into verse, not a merely conventional and artificially composed set picture. This seems to be a new voice, a new poetic personality in the making.

What one would not be able to miss in the poem is the elegiac quality, although the lament is for the conventionally lament-worthy, and the critics often like to make the claim that Byron is more modern than Wordsworth, someone aware in this poem of existing amid the ruins of civilisation, ironic and disenchanted. I think that one might have to agree with this as perhaps a plea for making Byron a more fashionable poet, not as a characterisation of any essential worth in Byron's verse. The trouble is that, simply, there are inconsistency and honesty, pathos and flamboyantly extravagant sentimental gestures all mixed up in the poem. It would be as wrong to dismiss the poem as theatrical self-indulgence as it would be to overpraise it for its honesty of reporting on situations, places and people, or its modernity. One has to take account of both the poetic sincerity and the awkward rhythm and phrasing, in sheer bad verse, of some of the perhaps sincere lamentations.

> On sloping mounds, or in the vale beneath,
> Are domes where whilome kings did make repair;
> But now the wild flowers round them only breathe;
> Yet ruin's splendour still is lying there.
>
> I, *xxii*

One has, nevertheless, to offset this sort of insincerity and candy-floss by the honesty of Byron's reporting at times. In Canto I Byron describes the Sierra Morena range which he passed through in late July 1809 on his way to Seville, as his footnote tells the reader. His stanza pays little attention to Spenser, but is a selection of eye-witnessed details:

> At every turn Morena's dusky height
> Sustains aloft the battery's iron load;
> And, far as mortal eye can compass sight,
> The mountain-howitzer, the broken road,
> The bristling palisade, the fosse o'er-flow'd,
> The station'd bands, the never-vacant watch,
> The magazine in rocky durance stow'd,
> The holster'd steed beneath the shed of thatch,
> The ball-piled pyramid, the ever-blazing match,
>
> I, *li*

We notice that these details are not a complete stanza or even a complete sentence, as we have to wait for the next stanza for its completion of sense with the verb for all those nouns in our stanza ('Portend the deeds to come:'). There are poeticisms which would never do for a newspaper report ('rocky durance'), but there is no manipulation of the facts of the situation; they are merely given to the reader. But, in the larger context, Byron tries to develop something like a theme, the theme of bravery and resolution against oppression and tyranny. So these details become one half of a statement, the second part of which is that Spain will inevitably be crushed by Napoleon. This is succeeded by a rhetorical 'And must they fall' questioning passage and the introduction of the Spanish heroine, the Maid of Saragoza. But do not think, says Byron next, that Spanish maids are a 'race of Amazons'; quite to the contrary, they are 'form'd for all the witching arts of love'. Now the 'theme' of bravery and tyranny fades away and 'Love' becomes important for a couple of stanzas, but it is a rather knowing young traveller who is pleased to condemn the 'paler dames' from the North:

> How poor their forms appear! how languid, wan, and weak!

He, of course, has travelled and is now well able to celebrate the ladies of the south, both Spaniard and Turk. Then there is no theme at all as Byron, in the act of writing all this, looks up from his lodging in Greece (though the poem has only got to Spain so far) and just cannot resist writing three stanzas on Parnassus.

> Oh, thou Parnassus! whom I now survey,
> Not in the phrenzy of a dreamer's eye,
> Not in the fabled landscape of a lay,
> But soaring snow-clad through thy native sky,
> In the wild pomp of mountain majesty!
> What marvel if I thus essay to sing?
> The humblest of thy pilgrims passing by
> Would gladly woo thine Echoes with his string,
> Though from thy heights no more one Muse will wave her wing.
>
> I, *lx*

Whether we are as impressed by the scene as Byron was, and whether the scene means as much to us as it did to Byron, it remains to say firmly that Byron is writing *au courant*, using the poem for various ends, no one of which would be by itself adequate to describe Cantos I and II exactly. This part of *Childe Harold's Pilgrimage* is, indeed, a romantic travelogue, tracing Byron's own journey and experiences (the fascination and the horror of the bullfight claim eleven stanzas in Canto I), but it is also a diary and the opportunity for the recording of personal thoughts, and an opportunity for public oratory on themes of public weight and worth: Death, Decay, Civilisation and so on. The result is that the reader is jostled along rather than

carefully guided through a meaningful meditation, and he is
not being driven along to a real goal for the pilgrimage, for
there is none.

But equally disconcerting is the way that Byron handles his
hero, the damned Gothic villain-hero. He presents him as a
contrast with the 'I' who has found it in his heart to celebrate
the ladies of Cadiz in I, *lxv*, and who exclaimed there:

> Ah, Vice! how soft are thy voluptuous ways!
> While boyish blood is mantling, who can 'scape
> The fascination of thy magic gaze?

The Childe, on the other hand, has gone a step beyond this
'fascination' and has come out on the other side of satiety:

> Yet to the beauteous form he was not blind,
> Though now it moved him as it moves the wise:
> Not that Philosophy on such a mind
> E'er deign'd to bend her chastely-awful eyes:
> But Passion raves itself to rest, or flies;
> And Vice, that digs her own voluptuous tomb,
> Had buried long his hopes, no more to rise:
> Pleasure's pall'd victim! life-abhorring gloom
> Wrote on his faded brow curst Cain's unresting doom.
>
> I, *lxxxiii*

And this, after the song that Byron makes him sing 'to Inez', is
the last we hear of him till Canto II. But if we think that we
have both the situation and the characteristics of these two
protagonists clear in our head then we are puzzled by Canto II.
There is a long passage there of meditation brought on by
Calypso's isles and concerned with Love, ending with the introduction of 'Sweet Florence'. Of course, she is none other than
Mrs. Spencer Smith of Byron's Malta stay, and the speaker
regrets his 'wayward, loveless heart' which is not worthy of
'thy shrine'. These are tender meditations and just not what one
might expect from the disillusioned Harold, though Byron tries
to swing them all on to him, and he has to be shown as invulner-
able to all Love's darts. But, if the sentimental and tender
reflections have been Harold's, despite the constant suggestions

of his being *un âme damné*, he would, nevertheless, seem a much more savoury character than the speaker. Poor Florence, it turns out, did not recognise the metal she was tampering with; she may have thought that she was dealing with 'a youth so raw', but not he. Despite appearances, he was dangerous, if only he had really bothered, but he did not.

> Little knew she that seeming marble heart,
> Now mask'd in silence or withheld by pride,
> Was not unskilful in the spoiler's art,
> And spread its snares licentious far and wide;
> Nor from the base pursuit had turn'd aside,
> As long as aught was worthy to pursue;
> But Harold on such arts no more relied;
> And had he doted on these eyes so blue,
> Yet never would he join the lover's whining crew.

II, *xxxiii*

Whatever we think of this, we do notice the moral term 'base' in 'base pursuit', and one might gather that the speaker was not going to let Harold escape scot free. But with this in mind the next two stanzas read very oddly. Briefly, they are cynical statements of a callous and calculating attitude to women as prey or of a world-weary rejection of Love. The knowingness of the stanza immediately following the 'spoiler's art' is striking; the speaker, out of his wisdom and experience, offers advice of the following order:

> Disguise ev'n tenderness, if thou are wise;
> Brisk Confidence still best with woman copes:
> Pique her and soothe in turn, soon Passion crowns thy hopes.

II, *xxxiv*

One might have expected this sort of thing from Harold, after what we have been led to believe of him, but this is the other speaker, the narrator Byron. An incoherent morality, a cynicism and an unpleasant knowingness lead into the reflection that the game is just not worth it anyway:

> When all is won that all desire to woo,
> The paltry prize is hardly worth the cost:

Youth wasted, minds degraded, honour lost,
These are thy fruits, successful Passion! these!

And then the poem switches swiftly so that we have no time to
sort out the attitudes in all of this, and Byron switches roles
and becomes the Nature poet and takes Harold more carefully
through Greece to Albania.

All we can really say, then, is that any attitude or mood that
seems to fit the situation, regardless of consistency or dramatic
continuity and credibility, is the one that Byron will adopt for
the moment.

Canto II is about Greece, opening with a rhetorical address to
the ancient deities of the country which is now suffering Turkish
rule. In the second stanza we can notice Byron escaping from
the chain of alliteration to a more rhythmically flowing style
and a more 'romantic':

The warrior's weapon and the sophist's stole
Are sought in vain, and o'er each mouldering tower,
Dim with the mist of years, gray flits the shade of power.

II, ii

This is 'romantic' in a simple pejorative sense, a fantasy situation
only loosely attached to any reality, a verse which asks for our
emotional sympathy by making us concentrate on the music
and the sound, entangling us in assonance (dim—mist—flits:
gray—shade). The image supporting the fantasy is firmly
enough stated, 'mouldering tower', but a time will come in
English poetry when there will be no supporting image, just the
metaphor standing unashamedly for all that has passed away.
Byron's handling of image and metaphor can, perhaps, be seen
very well in Stanza iv, a well-known reflection on the skull
with echoes of *Hamlet* almost inevitably, but with a prediction
of Yeats in its last two lines:

Yes, this was once Ambition's airy hall;
The dome of Thought, the palace of the Soul:
Behold through each lack-lustre, eyeless hole,
The gay recess of Wisdom and of Wit,
And Passion's host, that never brook'd control:
Can all saint, sage, or sophist ever writ,
People this lonely tower, this tenement refit?

This verse is dramatic and keeps the metaphor moving firmly and easily along, and even has a final couplet to stand back from the rest of the stanza and place the meditation in a context of the irretrievable, the irredeemable. Its plot, its movement of thought, is very like that of some Shakespearean sonnets, and some of Shakespeare's language is there too.

So, Byron's handling of verse is improving in Canto II, and he gets on so well that he's forgotten Harold until Stanza xvi:

> But where is Harold? shall I then forget
> To urge the gloomy wanderer o'er the wave?

But Harold needs no urging; there is nothing to hold him in Spain and he will do equally well in Greece:

> Hard is his heart whom charms may not enslave;
> But Harold felt not as in other times,
> And left without a sigh the land of war and crimes.

He submerges, however, until the 'Sweet Florence' passage already discussed, and Byron celebrates in a set-piece the energies and delights of a sea voyage. The poem catches fire under this set-piece and Byron springs into an immediacy, a here-and-nowness absent from the earlier stanzas:

> The moon is up; by Heaven, a lovely eye!
> Long streams of light o'er dancing waves expand;

II, *xxi*

and this introduces a long meditation encouraged by the physical isolation of ship-board with its independence of the past, its own special reality which may make us re-live our past:

> Thus bending o'er the vessel's laving side,
> To gaze on Dian's wave-reflected sphere,
> The soul forgets her schemes of hope and pride,
> And flies unconscious o'er each backward year.
> None are so desolate but something dear,
> Dearer than self, possesses or possess'd
> A thought, and claims the homage of a tear;
> A flashing pang! of which the weary breast
> Would still, albeit in vain, the heavy heart divest.

II, *xxiv*

John Galt, the novelist, from his observations of Byron on board the Townshend Packet in August 1809 going from Gibraltar to Malta, gives us the outsider's view of this meditation. Byron's habit in the evenings, according to Galt, was that

> when the lights were placed, he made himself a man forbid, took his station on the railing between the pegs on which the sheets are belayed and the shrouds, and there, for hours, sat in silence, enamoured, it may be, of the moon.

This is an example of Byron's so presenting an experience that the reader can entirely appreciate what the force of the experience was, but there are other passages where the reader can only really understand the significance of the original experience by having read the prose version of the same experience. He makes Childe Harold undergo his own experience of being driven ashore at night on an unknown part of the coast, and what becomes obvious is that the prose version gives the reality of fear and excitement, whereas the verse is much more generalised and moralising. In the letter to his mother of 12 November 1809, Byron writes:

> Two days ago I was nearly lost in a Turkish ship of war, owing to the ignorance of the captain and crew, though the storm was not violent. Fletcher yelled after his wife, the Greeks called on all the saints, the Mussulmans on Alla; the captain burst into tears and ran below deck, telling us to call on God; the sails were split, the main-yard shivered, the wind blowing fresh, the night setting in, and all our chance was to make Corfu, which is in possession of the French, or (as Fletcher pathetically termed it) 'a watery grave'. I did what I could to console Fletcher, but finding him incorrigible, wrapped myself up in my Albanian capote (an immense cloak), and lay down on deck to wait the worst. I have learnt to philosophise in my travels; and if I had not, complaint was useless. Luckily the wind abated, and only drove us on the coast of Suli, on the main land, where we landed, and proceeded, by the help of the natives, to Prevesa again; . . .

The verse keeps away from the personal and dramatic (though one can see that the detail of the stoicism and capote would be just the sort of telling detail for one of the later heroes in Byron's verse tales), and the stress falls on the kindness and humanity of the Suliotes who met the benighted travellers, and this suggests an 18th- rather than a 19th-century manner:

> Such conduct bears Philanthropy's rare stamp:
> To rest the weary and to soothe the sad,
> Doth lesson happier men, and shames at least the bad.

It is interesting to note in the same letter that Byron's mind is full of the many incidents of the journey, but cannot see that there is any coherence or pattern to them. Nor, I think, do they have a coherence in the verse, though Byron tries to display them as meaningful in moral or philosophical terms, but not in any thoroughgoing manner at all. It is obvious that some of the incidents impressed Byron and that is sufficient reason for their being presented in the poem. The wild energies of the Albanian troops, for example, are presented both because Byron is fascinated by any display of energy, and because the sight of their fierce dancing and the sound of their singing was a rarity for Europeans:

> In sooth it was no vulgar sight to see
> Their barbarous, yet their not indecent glee;

and the spectator is held enthralled by these magnificent, savage men:

> And, as the flames along their faces gleam'd,
> Their gestures nimble, dark eyes flashing free,
> The long wild locks that to their girdles stream'd,
> While thus in concert they this lay half sang, half screamed:—
>
> II, *lxxii*

and we are treated to a translation of a rousing robber song, celebrating war, destruction and Ali Pasha. But, typical of the way this poem moves from attitude to attitude, Byron moves into a lament immediately for the lost glory of ancient Greece and the miserable state of the modern Greeks in an attempt to rouse them into activity to throw off the Turkish yoke. But he quite soon leaves this theme and modulates into a description

54

of the Greek revels at Carnival in Istanbul, not as any attempt to show a contrast for the worse with the robber song, but because it is just as interesting to Byron, another of the sensations which gave him pleasure. Stanzas lxxx to lxxxiii ask the reader to admire the 'sensibility' of the creator of this setting for Love; the scene is theatrical enough with echo, measured oar, rippling waters, moonlight, breeze and sparkling billows, and forms the backcloth for young Love.

> While many a languid eye and thrilling hand
> Exchanged the look few bosoms may withstand,
> Or gently prest, return'd the pressure still:
> Oh Love! young Love! bound in thy rosy band,
> Let sage or cynic prattle as he will,
> These hours, and only these, redeem Life's years of ill!
>
> II, *lxxxi*

This not only makes an odd contrast with the admired war-like energies of the Albanian soldiers, the shouts about the Greeks as slavish sufferers under Turkish domination, but also the thoughts about women and Love seen earlier with their cynicism and knowingness. But there are some who

> . . . loathe the laughter idly loud
> And long to change the robe of revel for the shroud!

and this leads equally well into shame once more at the modern degeneracy. This time, though, that sort of thought melts into the sentimentality of feeling the beautiful sadness of old ruins where

> . . . strangers only not regardless pass,
> Lingering like me, perchance, to gaze, and sigh 'Alas!'

So the melancholy chimes in with both the landscape and the human heart, and Byron sounds like a high-class travel agent urging the quality of the experiences to be gained by the sensitive pilgrim. The contemporary reader might have been expected to enjoy the 'sensitive' scene-painting of Greece, a generalised scene, literary in its demand on the reader's love of the classics, and his respect for the golden age of Greek civilisation.

Yet are thy skies as blue, thy crags as wild;
Sweet are thy groves, and verdant are thy fields,
Thine olive ripe as when Minerva smiled,
And still his honey'd wealth Hymettus yields;
There the blithe bee his fragrant fortress builds,
The freeborn wanderer of thy mountain-air;
Apollo still thy long, long summer gilds,
Still in his beam Mendeli's marbles glare;
Art, Glory, Freedom fail, but Nature still is fair.

II, *lxxxvii*

But the historic past recalls the personal past, and the loneliness of the ruins and monumental memories of the landscape are analogues of the loneliness of this traveller, his existence as a ruin left behind by all those he loved, now unhappily all dead. All that remains for him now is Death. And on that melodramatic note Canto II ends.

There are several things that strike one about Canto II. One is that the poem progresses by spiralling, that is to say that any attempt to display the 'themes' would show the slightness of the material being worked upon and also the way that these are constantly returned to. The poem is not evolving, but ruminative, meditative, centring about 'my' responses to Greece, its past glory, its present slavishness and the co-presence of beauty and sadness. All this, of course, is an emblem of the spiritual state of 'I', whose past glory is Love and whose present dereliction the death of Love.

Although we would want to connect the poem with the old loco-descriptive poem, we would have to make the point that this is a poem which confesses all, which concentrates upon the observer and his reflections. These reflections matter now because they are specially personal and not general moral reflections. But we must be careful here and recognise the split between the calmly observant eye of the picturesque traveller and the self-absorbed eye of the love-lorn 'I', and again between these two and Childe Harold himself, the man of ennui, the satiated and cynical traveller, constantly twitching himself to be off and away. The trouble is, though, that these may be distinguishable on reflection but they all tend to run together and blur into one another in the poem.

With the spiralling or digressive nature of the poem we must see how Byron uses his own experiences. There are the actual experiences of which we have prose parallels in his letters, reflections on these events which may be seen as occurring at the same time as the events, and there are contemporary reflections on past events. Finally, a contemporary situation may be built into a work really devoted to a past set of experiences: 'I', in the here-and-now, am experiencing *this*, but also remembering *that*. This complex act points to the final way of writing in Byron's omnium gatherum poem, *Don Juan*, and it makes one wonder about the central figure who is not the 'hero'. The 'hero' is a convenient aid if anything, a peg on whom Byron can hang reflections and moral pronouncements, a way of tapping off some of his own moods and responses, but there are times when the reader is just not sure who is saying what. The reader who knows *Don Juan* can perhaps see *Childe Harold* as a pointer to Byron's later attempt to explore the nature of 'I', a more philosophical exploration.

One imagines that one of the reasons for the success of the poem on its publication is that there is something here for everyone: sensibility for the 'sensibilitous' and fashionable; courage-inspiring reflection for the man at ease; love expressed in a novelistic way, that is hands/hearts/bosoms but innocent of actual sex; and a ravaged heart (asking for pity and soothing) with classics thrown in for the classic-bred.

5

Fictional Biography

Following on the immediate and electrifying success of Childe
Harold as a popular damned hero, Byron wrote a number of
stories in verse. These were mainly centred round the places that
he had known on his tour, Greece, Albania, Turkey and so on;
the mysterious East. This part of the world had held literary
fascination for English readers ever since the first translation of
the *Arabian Nights* between 1704 and 1712, and there were at
least two well-known practitioners of the East in literature in
Byron's time, Moore and Southey. Both of these writers had
treated and were treating the East as the scene of magic and
romance, the embroidered tall story with spices and bulbuls as
essential ingredients. Byron had actually been there and had
seen that this was a locale not simply of local colour but of raw
passions, excitement and danger. These were to be his ingredients, and he was equally at pains to get any physical detail or
historical allusion correct. He had not travelled simply as a tourist,
but as a discoverer, though the truths he brought home with
him from the Levant were, no doubt, those that struck *him*
most forcibly.

But it was not simply the story, such as it was, that was his
dominant interest in any of these verse tales. Some of them are
not really tales at all, but are opportunities for Byron to erect a
situation which will enable him to get something down on to
paper which will exorcise his own difficulties of one kind or
another, emotional or psychological, without being confessional
poems. They will exteriorise, in one way or another, Byron's
own conflicts. The drama will be a self-dramatising; the protagonists will, in the end, turn out to be single and not several.

Byron wrote the poems with great rapidity, of which he was inordinately proud (it put him amongst the class of English writers who were gentlemen first and poet-amateurs, not your ink-stained professional) and he pays the price of this speed. His writing is often slipshod, uncorrected and unsubtle, his structures often chaotic and his style banal. But there are gains: his verse is much more direct, leaner and less inclined to narcissism, and there is usually a rapidity of relating incidents which makes for rapid reading on the reader's part as it was the product of rapid writing on the author's.

It is possible to lump all these poems together, *The Giaour, The Corsair, Lara, The Bride of Abydos, The Siege of Corinth* and *Parisina,* and to talk about the common elements of plot, characterisation, values and Byron's attitude, simply because they are all, to a greater or lesser extent, variations on a single story with a single hero. One can say that the common situation is this: there is a splendidly aristocratic figure who has been corrupted from good to evil, largely by events beyond his own control, a natural leader of men, though basically an independent figure, at odds with others, someone with an unshakable pride, ungovernable passions and a ravaged heart. Yet he has an undying love for one woman, whether she be alive or dead, and this is meant to be one of his pleasantly attractive features, though it must be said that all of his qualities seem to be intended as splendid and admirable. One says *seems* because what is increasingly obvious about the tales is that Byron is wholeheartedly on the side of his hero, if not inside his skin.

It is usual to say that there is no moral scheme within the tales by which actions and situations can be criticised, and this seems to be true. They are, in a very real sense, personal and private poems which Byron is writing in two ways. He is exploiting his own emotional states, and he is trying to externalise something of himself in a fictional form. Consequently, if he is not simply to write autobiography, but to render private experiences, whether real or those of his own fantasies (and there seems no reason to deny the element of fantasy in them), he has to hide, as far as he can, the realities within the story. This means that when he is translating a private situation into his fiction he must create an air of mystery about the reasons for actions; to give credible reasons for action, often of a most unusual sort, would demand that he create a whole fiction, an imitation of a set of real actions. But this would be to write with far more care and with far more attention to the artefact, the literary product. These poems are metaphors rather than fully independent tales with their own inner logic and coherence. We are far too dependent on the author's whim for that. Byron sometimes did not know what the outcome of his tales would be, and one can see, when one is reading a particular tale, that the story could have gone in several different directions, or that the author is, rather highhandedly, suddenly shifting the way the story is moving as he gets an idea and starts to work it out.

We can examine one of the tales and treat it as representative: *The Giaour* was written in the spring of 1813, though this was only about 400 lines, and the poem grew during the year until it reached 1334 lines in the autumn. As we now have it Byron pretends that it is really not a unit but some 'disjointed fragments' of a tale set in a more riotous and tumultuous past, as he says in the *Advertisement*. But this will not do. There are too many relators of the story to enable it to have any narrative coherence. It is usual to say that there are three narrators, a Moslem fisherman, a monk and the Giaour himself. But there is a fourth, Byron, or the introducer. And this fourth does not merely complicate the narration, he introduces his own particular interests in the locale, Greece—notably the situation of a subjected Greece, the past glory that was Greece and the present destruction of that Eden. One can see a possible scheme for the poem, a metaphoric scheme and not a narrative plot, in the way that the poem gets under way. There is a long first verse paragraph (after the initial six lines which simply mourn Themistocles, the man who saved the land in vain), which celebrates Greece in terms of an Eden or Arabic paradise:

> For there the Rose, o'er crag or vale,
> Sultana of the Nightingale,

> The maid for whom his melody,
>   His thousand songs are heard on high,
> Blooms blushing to her lover's tale:

This physical paradise was, of course, destroyed by a 'Tyrant', man. I should say that this is an example of the fuzziness of Byron's argument; he means to offer a paradise which man destroys:

> There man, enamour'd of distress,
> Should mar it into wilderness,
> And trample, brute-like o'er each flower
> That tasks not one laborious hour. . . .

and this is understandable, but he fuses the primeval destruction with the present political domination of Turk over Greek, and we have the political term 'tyrants' thrown in at the end of the passage:

> So soft the scene, so form'd for joy,
> So curst the tyrants that destroy!

Then the notion of Greece as a dead woman killed by the tyrant is taken up in the next passage, but now the tyrant is also Death itself: when the gazer on the corpse of the dead woman could perhaps wonder if she were truly dead or not:

> Some moments, ay, one treacherous hour,
> He still might doubt the tyrant's power.

What might just conceivably have followed would have been a specific example of someone subjected to tyranny, someone who is to mourn, eventually, the death at the hands of the tyrant, his beautiful loved one. That is, we might have seen the preamble about paradise and Greece (both as paradise and woman) as setting the tone and the outcome, tragic and inevitable under this scheme, of the individual Giaour.

But no. We are to get more used to Byron's rapidity of movement, both of verse and thought, that we must be swept along without seeing structure in this way. So, after the two passages discussed he can digress into one of the Childe Harold themes, the debasement of modern Greeks:

The hearts within thy valleys bred,
The fiery souls that might have led
   Thy sons to deeds sublime,
Now crawl from cradle to the grave,
Slaves—nay, the bondsmen of a slave,
   And callous save to crime.

And then Byron can really start the story of *The Giaour*, after
168 lines which might have been made operative within the
poem, instead of being mood setting, allowing opportunities for
Byron to follow his favourite thoughts wherever they would
lead him.

Once we are engaged with the story proper we are jostled
from point of view to point of view, from sea to shore, from
the fisherman to someone with an omniscience, the narrator.
The fisherman quite certainly could witness the scene and ask
questions like:

Who thundering comes on blackest steed,
With slacken'd bit and hoof of speed?

Though, even then, one might ask questions as this is a night-
scene and yet one has both the visual detail and its admiration
in 'blackest steed', but one is perhaps more worried about who
can see or know:

Though weary waves are sunk to rest,
There's none within his rider's breast;
And though tomorrow's tempest lower,
'Tis calmer than thy heart, young Giaour!

And then, even though we have a hostile witness in the Turkish
fisherman, we certainly have a discerning one, and an admirer
perforce:

I know thee not, I loathe thy race,
But in thy lineaments I trace
What Time shall strengthen, not efface:
Though young and pale, that shallow front
Is scathed by fiery's passion's brunt;

and then we are back both in story-time past with the fisherman's announcing how much the sight of the horseman reverberated in his memory. Without warning, then, we switch to the historic present tense to follow the Giaour's progress along the shore. We are given experience and knowledge which, we might think, must be denied to the fisherman, but he is an extraordinary one by any standard. Consider the hyperbole of the couplet which is interpolated into the verse description of the rider's movements;

> And not a star but shines too bright
> On him who takes such timeless flight.

Then the succeeding passage lets us hear a voice even more perceptive than our fisherman, someone more intimate in his knowledge of feelings and psychology:

> 'Twas but a moment that he stood,
> Then sped as if by death pursued;
> But in that instant o'er his soul
> Winters of Memory seem'd to roll,
> And gather in that drop of time
> A life of pain, an age of crime.

Our suspicion that we are going to know the causes of this interesting psychological condition is baseless, however; the glass clouds again, and what might have been the substance of that momentous moment is veiled under the extravagances of:

> For infinite as boundless space
> The thought that Conscience must embrace,
> Which in itself can comprehend
> Woe without name, or hope, or end.

This, of course, leads us back into damnation, but of Satanic proportions (and grandeur), certainly much bigger and more impressive than our own niggling guilts.

Then the situation is shot back into a far distant past, analogous to the distant past of the prologue, and we have a lament for the decay of 'Hassan's hall', and we see the Giaour as the avenger, the 'curse for Hassan's sin'. The lament is very like some written for *Hours of Idleness*, and cadences like the following ring a bell:

For the stream has shrunk from its marble bed,
Where the weeds and the desolate dust are spread.

This lament, apparently from Turkish lips, presumably the
fisherman's, has the same status as the lament for Greece, and
the notion of politically taking sides in the poem is wavering.
Though, on another count, the verse is not as impressive as the
lament for Greece and has not the same emotional pressures
behind it (there is not the burning anger, for example), and it
ends with such a bathos that Greece may be said, perhaps, to
win the day:

The guest flies the hall, and the vassal from labour,
Since his turban was cleft by the infidel's sabre!

Again, the story leaps forward, or backward, into an historic
present where we are on the shore again with an inspection of
Moslem face by Moslem face, conversation, trust and mistrust,
and the carrying of something for dumping out at sea, with all
the 'secrets' now hidden in its depths.

Then outside the story again in the abstracted pictorial world
of the literary East, as in the prologue. Here we have some sort
of a moralist drawing out the analogy between the butterfly (in
Kashmeer) and its young pursuer with Beauty and the 'full-
grown child' pursuing it. Both are 'victims', and we see the
relationship to the previous passage about what was dumped
out at sea only at the end:

And lovelier things have mercy shown
To every failing but their own,
And every woe a tear can claim
Except an erring sister's shame.

But we have to be skilled to see the relationship, or at least we
have to know or remember the famous incidents of women
being tied in sacks to be dumped out at sea for crimes against
sexual regularity.

But before we can return to the story by this indirect route,
we have a more powerful few lines of verse which develop
another analogy, that of the 'Mind, that broods o'er guilty woes',

64

being like the 'Scorpion girt by fire', and the reader now sees this as belonging essentially to the Giaour, both by its intensity and its siting. He also wonders what is the guilty relationship between the woman and the Giaour; lover or murderer? In fact, it will turn out that he will accuse himself of being both; though her lover, he has been the indirect cause of her death, and this is his guilt. But for the moment we rest content with the metaphysics:

> So writhes the mind Remorse hath riven,
> Unfit for earth, undoom'd for heaven,
> Darkness above, despair beneath,
> Around it flame, within it death!

Needless to say, this could stand as a motto for several, if not all, the verse tales.

We return to the story with our being told in a few lines, by a Moslem voice, the story of Leila, her husband Hassan and her death, and the voice celebrates her beauty in extravagant terms, putting Hassan outside both Christian sympathies (he's an enemy) and also outside the sympathies of his more perceptive Moslem colleagues. Then into a story past tense with a ballad-like opening, interesting to note:

> Stern Hassan hath a journey ta'en
> With twenty vassals in his train, . . .

to lead into the immediacy of a present tense for the journey of the brigands and their ambush by the Giaour and his men, with a verse which rides swiftly along enjoying the physical clash and the excitement. But attention is deflected into an extended simile of the clash between the two enemies as the meeting of a river and the sea; and this is meant as a way of placing the implacability of the hatred and as indicating the mutual physical destruction. Just as they have 'mutual wrong', so they are 'true foes' and

> Friends meet to part; Love laughs at faith;
> True foes, once met, are join'd till death.

Then the ambush and the fight and Hassan is seen to die, and the Giaour given a speech which gives *us* his reasons for joining a raiding band, because we must not think of him as some ordinary pirate:

> I watch'd my time, I leagued with these,
> The traitor in his turn to seize;
> My wrath is wreak'd, the deed is done,
> And now I go—but go alone.

We now turn to Hassan's mother awaiting impatiently her son's return from a journey to marry a new wife, but, ironically, she hears that he has 'wed' a 'fearful bride'. A lamenting Moslem voice celebrates Hassan and predicts a Moslem heaven for brave men:

> Who falls in battle 'gainst a Giaour
> Is worthiest an immortal bower.

A similar, or perhaps the same, Moslem voice continues after a gap in the text with a curse on the 'false Infidel'; this is no simple curse, but one made 'shocking' by wishing vampirism on him, with associations with incest and a modulation into pathos for 'the youngest, most beloved of all' who must fall for the father's crime, and this must be a daughter (if only, one imagines, because Byron never had a son). One imagines that this predicted death of a daughter fits the whole series of feminine catastrophes—Greece, Leila and now the daughter. The trouble is, though, that this is all we hear of her, and we next meet the Giaour as a guest of a monastery where he has been for the last six years, and there is no further mention of a daughter. But he has not changed since the first speaker first saw him, and on seeing him he says that the Giaour's face

> . . . breathes the same dark spirit now,
> As death were stamp'd upon his brow.

True to this face, and to the spirit of the Byronic hero, his Christianity, such as it is, is confined to his 'face' (complexion) and he will have nothing to do with 'our holy shrine', says a monk to the Moslem.

66

After that introduction to the Giaour in the monastery we have an all-knowing voice telling of the 'dark and unearthly' scowl, and the 'nameless spell' of his mesmeric eye:

> As if that eye and bitter smile
> Transferr'd to others fear and guile;

and we hear of his essential, but blighted, nobility of soul:

> The common crowd but see the gloom
> Of wayward deeds, and fitting doom;
> The close observer can espy
> A noble soul, and lineage high.

To complete this idealised self-portrait we have the comparison of the noble soul in decay compared to a ruined Gothic tower (like Newstead Abbey, one imagines):

> Each ivied arch, and pillar lone,
> Pleads haughtily for glories gone!

This celebratory voice continues with a description of the doomed man, now a monk in everything but prayer and worship, but, oddly enough, the verse suddenly becomes personal and talks of monkish dress as 'our garb'. Though no monk could have spoken with such an intimate Byronic knowledge if he were simply an observer, we have to get on with the tale and try not to notice such discrepancies, and here the pace of the verse could carry a none too careful reader over easily enough.

Following this we have a moralist's voice, one we have not heard from for some time, reflecting on passionate love and its relation to 'sterner hearts':

> Thus passion's fire, and woman's art,
> Can turn and tame the sterner heart;

a doctrine later due for some refinement and modification. After a gap a parallel reflection takes place, this time on the emptiness and lifelessness of the state of 'remorse':

> The keenest pangs the wretched find
>   Are rapture to the dreary void,
> The leafless desert of the mind,
>   The waste of feelings unemployed.

And one sees why the critic must, in some way or other, talk about Byron's identifying himself with his hero, or projecting himself into his hero, because in this sort of passage one cannot tell the teller from the tale. The image is one which recurs so constantly in Byron's more disillusioned poems and letters that one sees it as a Byronic commonplace, equally at home in personal lyric or imported into what does not seem to be so personal (but really is) in the tales. (As an example we might simply quote the second stanza of his last lyric *On This Day I Complete my Thirty-Sixth Year*:

> My days are in the yellow leaf;
>   The flowers and fruits of love are gone;
> The worm, the canker, and the grief
>   Are mine alone.)

And in this poem we might well ask who would think of imagery of 'A lonely wreck on fortune's shore' and its being

> Better to sink beneath the shock
> Than moulder piecemeal on the rock

but the Byronic Giaour, whereas it seems to be an impersonal commentator.

From here until the end of the poem, about 355 lines, apart from a six-line coda, the Giaour speaks, addressing a monk. He gives a self-proclamation and proclaims his values, perfecting his stance as a Byronic hero. He has 'passions fierce and uncontroll'd', and is a man who

> still in hours of love or strife
> I've 'scaped the weariness of life:

and he certainly does not declare himself a coward:

> My spirit shrunk not to sustain
> The searching throes of ceaseless pain;

in fact, a Satanic figure. If not Satanic, then at least cursed with a curse almost as ancient in biblical terms, the mark of Cain:

> But look—'tis written on my brow!
> There read of Cain the curse and crime,
> In characters unworn by time:

68

because he was the murderer, indirectly, of his loved one. Byron
is trying to equate Hassan and the Giaour, as both had the same
attitude to false love, and both loved Leila, but the verse dissolves
in such bathos that I do not think quite equalled in the rest of
the poem:

> Yet did he but what I had done
> Had she been false to more than one,
> Faithless to him, he gave the blow;
> But true to me, I laid him low.

Now the new Byronic hero has to repudiate the sort of love-
lyric that Byron himself had composed earlier, and this new ideal
is a passion which is uncontrollable, a 'lava flood/That boils in
Aetna's breast of flame', but which has a constancy, superseding
death and all categories of human value:

> My good, my guilt, my weal, my woe,
> My hope on high—my all below . . .
> . . . thou wert, thou art
> The cherish'd madness of my heart.

Let the friend of pre-Leila days, who prophesied the Giaour's
doom, now see what he has grown into; and the autumnal leaf
image comes round again, with a more distinct echo of *Macbeth*
this time:

> The wither'd frame, the ruin'd mind,
> The wrack by passion left behind,
> A shrivell'd scroll, a scatter'd leaf,
> Sear'd by the autumn blast of grief!

And he ends his tale with recounting a vision where he saw the
dead Leila coming to him and also, as ghosts will, beckoning
him to follow her. Having apparently, in the gap between this
passage and the next, which are his last few words, given the
monk his name and having revealed all, he wishes for an un-
marked grave without 'name or emblem'. The mystery about
him still remains for the reader, and this is characteristic of
Byron's tale-telling, where more must be hinted and suspected
than is told, where rhetorical questions for central issues are more

powerful agents than simple factual narrative, where the aura is so important. And, true to this, the reader is puzzled by wondering who says the epilogue; it is not the monk whom the Giaour addressed, nor is it the Moslem whom we have met earlier, but another communal voice, the voice of the people who keep alive this tale:

> This broken tale was all we knew
> Of her he loved, or him he slew.

But the tale is so obviously an artefact, with its swift ranging through time, from present to past to distant past, from voice to voice, from known to unknown, that the reader recognises a tale deliberately told to arouse interest and intensity; to be confusing it is often confused. What one might say is that, despite the uncertainties I have outlined of voice and situation, the manner of narration makes both for the reader's interest and fascination, with the clues being followed up sometimes and sometimes left sterile to make for the reader's puzzlement and continuing interest (for as long as the tale is told). The analogy I would offer is that of detective fiction, where the reader is only gradually enlightened and is made to suspect *this* and forget *that* as he moves along in the work. That is, at least, we must see *The Giaour* as a work of entertainment, as something which offers an escape from the known world of fixities and trivia into a splendid world of enduring and ungovernable passion, of crime and guilt, of violence, of ravage and exotic splendour, with a modern Satanic hero lovingly handled by his creator.

6

'Childe Harold's Pilgrimage' III & IV

In 1816 when Byron left England he left behind his estranged wife and his daughter, his beloved half-sister Augusta, his four years of pinnacle fame and his hatred of English society and English hypocrisy. He took with him a personal agony and an increased awareness of poetry as an idealising medium, poetry as 'a heavenly hue of words, like sunbeams'.

Taking up *Childe Harold's Pilgrimage* again, he brought his agony and disillusionment to bear in his writing, and one can almost say that the Childe is replaced quite simply by Byron. This is not strictly true, but the Childe fades into Byron much more perceptively in this canto than ever before, and we can see him more and more speaking in his own voice about his own situation and experiences. Looking back on the 'Tale' as so far written he found that it all seemed sterile and from a far distant past whose only relationship to the present was a continuing and increasing aridity. Byron's syntax is often unclear, but that seems to be one way of taking

> in that Tale I find
> The furrows of long thought, and dried-up tears,
> Which, ebbing, leave a sterile track behind,
> O'er which all heavily the journeying years
> Plod the last sands of life,—where not a flower appears.
>
> III, *iii*

Now the act of writing the poem appears as partly therapeutic in that it will 'wean me from the weary dream/Of selfish grief or sadness', and partly as a way of increasing the spent life of the writer. Stanza vi is a justly famous one and is a memorable statement of this particular view of literature:

'Tis to create, and in creating live
A being more intense, that we endow
With form our fancy, gaining as we give
The life we image, even as I do now.
What am I? Nothing: but not so art thou,
Soul of my thought! with whom I traverse earth,
Invisible but gazing, as I glow
Mix'd with thy spirit, blended with thy birth,
And feeling still with thee in my crush'd feelings dearth.

The Childe has changed, and though he is still for the moment recognisably Harold, and perhaps more recognisably Byron, he has tempered some of his gloom but increased his despair:

With nought of hope left, but with less of gloom;
The very knowledge that he lived in vain,
That all was over on this side the tomb,
Had made Despair a smilingness assume.

III, *xvi*

And so, Harold-Byron comes to Waterloo and one of Byron's finest set-pieces. In addition to the high-toned meditation on the Childe Harold theme of *vanitas vanitatum* and *sic transit gloria mundi* which one has grown accustomed to in I and II, we have a dramatic recreation of the eve of the Battle of Waterloo. Byron chooses the ball-room and its glamour and romance, an index of beauty and youth in its fitting setting, but also as an ironically ideal setting for slaughter. Byron manages rhythms and tones very well, bringing out a poignancy and a bitter-sweetness from the situation. He can avoid moral reflection here as he has introduced the scene with a typical 'reflection' on the battlefield:

Ambition's life and labours all were vain:
He wears the shatter'd links of the world's broken chain.

III, *xviii*

Byron's emotions go out to the young men and women torn asunder by the brutality and senselessness of war, and to the brave soldiers who die the inevitable death. The Scottish contingent have a stanza of praise (*xxvi*), but they, like the others, are doomed, and Byron's melancholy has far more resonance and force when one remembers the triviality of the laments of the *Hours of Idleness* volume:

> And Ardennes waves above them her green leaves,
> Dewy with nature's tear-drops as they pass,
> Grieving, if aught inanimate e'er grieves,
> Over the unreturning brave,—alas!
> Ere evening to be trodden like the grass
> Which now beneath them, but above shall grow
> In its next verdure, when this fiery mass
> Of living valour, rolling on the foe
> And burning with high hope shall moulder cold and low.
>
> III, *xxvii*

Lament for the dead leads into a long meditation on the broken survival of life, the heart shattered like a mirror, the survivor of disaster 'withering on' . . . 'till all without is old'. This, in turn, leads into an analysis of Napoleon, an obvious analogue for Byron himself, a man whose fame and potential were of the highest, now at his lowest ebb. Both men, if one reads a little between the lines, meet fortune's turn with an aristocratic aloofness:

> Yet well thy soul hath brook'd the turning tide
> With that untaught innate philosophy,
> Which, be it wisdom, coldness, or deep pride,
> Is gall and wormwood to an enemy.
>
> III, *xxxix*

One recognises the characteristics of the Byronic hero down on his luck, and Napoleon is understood Byronically, and he turns out to be another of the series of heroes, almost as though he deserves to be set in an oriental tale:

> there is a fire
> And a motion of the soul which will not dwell
> In its own narrow being, but aspire
> Beyond the fitting medium of desire,
> And, but once kindled, quenchless evermore,
> Preys upon high adventure, nor can tire
> Of aught but rest; a fever at the core,
> Fatal to him who bears, to all who ever bore.   III, *xlii*

There might be something here centrally important to an understanding of Napoleon's psychology, but Napoleon and all aspirants to the unconquered heights are left for what is now presented as 'True Wisdom', which is either an ideal state or presented through Nature. As Harold stands on the banks of the 'majestic Rhine' he

> gazes on a work divine,
> A blending of all beauties; streams and dells,
> Fruit, foliage, crag, wood, cornfield, mountain, vine,
> And chiefless castles breathing stern farewells
> From gray but leafy walls, where Ruin greenly dwells.
>
> III, *xlvi*

Here Harold-Byron sees Nature, the Rhine, as beautiful and maintaining its present beauty in despite of the 'thousand battles' which have taken place on its banks. Of course, it cannot obliterate other memories than its own, but it is still beautiful and Harold-Byron is 'not insensible' to the simple beauty. And now, against all the supposed evidence about Harold-Byron and the exhausted passion and dead heart, we learn that there was 'one soft breast'

> Which unto his was bound by stronger ties
> Than the church binds withal; and, though unwed,
> *That* love was pure, and, far above disguise,
> Had stood the test of mortal enmities
> Still undivided, and cemented more
> By peril, dreaded most in female eyes; . . .
>
> III, *lv*

And so the biographies of Harold and Byron come so close in their particulars, not simply generically as so often in the past, that there are four interpolated stanzas on the Rhine as a tribute to and private gift for the loved one left behind, Augusta (though no names are mentioned, of course). The Rhine passage closes with memories of 'Freedom's champion', the Frenchman Marceau, and of the siege-resisting fortress of Ehrenbreitstein, and the final reflection that

74

could the ceaseless vultures cease to prey
On self-condemning bosoms, it were here,
Where Nature, nor too sombre nor too gay,
Wild but not rude, awful yet not austere,
Is to the mellow Earth as Autumn to the year.

III, *lix*

This oscillation between the private grief made public and celebration of the scenery in narrative terms continues by way of Morat and further reflection on war and the levelled pride of human hands, the wreck of years, and 'deeds which should not pass away' until we arrive at Lake Leman and Geneva. Here we have Byron's reflection on Byronic loneliness, a stage which comes after both the 'wretched interchange of wrong for wrong/Midst a contentious world, striving where none are strong', and the 'fatal penitence' which ensues from this. The odd thing is that Byron's exclamations about being alone now have a different note; 'And love Earth only for its earthly sake' turns out to be a pastiche of Shelley and Wordsworth in *lxxi–lxxv*. Echoes of Wordsworth's vocabulary and attitudes are impossible to miss, and one could notice, say, *lxxii*:

I live not in myself, but I become
Portion of that around me; and to me
High mountains are a feeling, but the hum
Of human cities torture: I can see
Nothing to loathe in nature, save to be
A link reluctant in a fleshly chain,
Class'd among creatures, when the soul can flee,
And with the sky, the peak, the heaving plain
Of ocean, or the stars, mingle, and not in vain.

Of course, this is not purely quotation from Wordsworth, and it is clear that Byron is not really holding just those views of man's relationship with nature which characterise Wordsworth. Wordsworth must have heard his own voice, or at least echoes of his voice drifting through the verse, because Moore recorded conversations with Wordsworth on Byron's supposed plagiarisms. Moore's memory of a conversation goes as follows:

> . . . the whole third canto of 'Childe Harold' founded on his style and sentiments. The feeling of natural objects which is there expressed, not caught by B. from nature herself, but from him (Wordsworth), and spoiled in the transmission. 'Tintern Abbey' the source of it all . . .
>
> MEMOIRS III, 161

We can balance this with the other reported conversation, this time Byron's with Medwin:

> Shelley, when I was in Switzerland, used to dose me with Wordsworth physic to nausea: and I do remember then reading some things of his with pleasure.
>
> MEDWIN II, 40

The truth seems to be that whatever came into the poetry for the first time now was under the guidance and influence of Shelley whom Byron spent a great deal of time with while he stayed in Geneva and whose conversations must have made a great impression on him. Byron, at any rate, expresses a much more idealistic response to nature than ever before (or ever again) and we must also bear in mind the proximity of the memory of Rousseau. Geneva and the lake inevitably bring him to Byron's mind, and he becomes another Byronic *alter ego*. Rousseau is celebrated as the 'apostle of affliction', 'he who threw/Enchantment over passion', and especially as an idealist artist:

> But his was not the love of living dame,
> Nor of the dead who rise upon our dreams,
> But of ideal beauty, which became
> In him existence, and o'erflowing teems
> Along his burning page, distemper'd though it seems.
>
> III, *lxxviii*

Rousseau is seen as laying the foundations of a new world, unhappily not yet come to pass, but possible; the Revolution misfired, but the time will come. Passion, Rousseau and Byron are all then submerged in a night-piece by the placid lake, whose stillness warns against the wild world, distraction and the roar of the ocean, a night-piece written by the new Byron nature poet with his ears hearing the voice of the lake sounding 'sweet as if a Sister's voice reproved'. This passage much impressed Sir Walter Scott when he reviewed the poem in the *Quarterly Review* in 1816, though he sees it in a rather old-fashioned way:

> The poem proceeds to describe, in a tone of great beauty and feeling, a night-scene witnessed on the Lake of Geneva; and each natural object, from the evening grasshopper to the stars, 'the poetry of heaven,' suggests the contemplation of the connection between the Creator and his works.

Byron certainly starts in his new voice with

> From the high host
> Of stars, to the lull'd lake and mountain-coast,
> All is concenter'd in a life intense,
> Where not a beam, nor air, nor leaf is lost,
> But hath a part of being, and a sense
> Of that which is of all Creator and defence.

III, lxxxix

The echo does seem to be of Wordsworth's *Tintern Abbey*, but Byron cannot hold on to any man's idealism, even Wordsworth's or Shelley's, for very long. It is a different sort of Nature which he describes in the following stanzas, a storm in an impressive countryside of mountains and the 'swift Rhone'. The energy of the storm excites him, as it has always done; it calls to him, but it is not a part of him nor he of it. The natural exists in its own right, and can be used by the maker of poems as an analogue of the human mind, the human heart, a most old-fashioned and unWordsworthian view. Addressing 'Sky, mountains, river, winds, lake, lightnings', he exclaims:

> the far roll
> Of your departing voices, is the knoll
> Of what in me is sleepless,—if I rest.
> But where of ye, O tempests! is the goal?
> Are ye like those within the human breast?
> Or do ye find, at length, like eagles, some high nest?

III, xcvi

Enthralled by the energy of the storm, the poet thinks that if all that he was or knew or felt could be uttered in a single word, that word would be *Lightning*, a typically theatrical and Byronic word, one might have thought:

> But as it is, I live and die unheard,
> With a most voiceless thought, sheathing it as a sword.
>
> III, *xcvii*

But, with the storm over, and the one word unspeakable, the poem comes slowly down to earth and Byron himself. We have a meditation on Clarens as the abode of love, consecrated by Rousseau, and Lausanne and Ferney, the places associated with Voltaire and Gibbon; meditation in the manner demanded by the loco-descriptive tradition which Byron is continuing in this poem. Byron looks out from his page as he writes ('This page, which from my reveries I feed,/Until it seems prolonging without end'), and we recognise that there is not the moral fervour which one associates with the older loco-descriptive poetry, but a man allowing his mind to rest on this and that object in the landscape in order that he may not think about himself, a quite different approach from that of the meditative poem. And so, after reflection on the Italy that he can see in the distance, Byron goes into the confessional and gives us again the reasons for writing, 'to steel/The heart against itself', setting himself up once more as the aloof, crowd-hating aristocrat (with the inevitable echo of *Macbeth*—'Had I not filed my mind, which thus itself subdued'), but ending with an address to his infant daughter. Harold is clearly abandoned and this address utters Byron's hope that the child will, despite all efforts to breed hate for him in her, come to love him and hear his voice through his poetry. *We* can certainly hear Byron's 'very self and voice' speaking here with accents of love and mingled bitterness. He holds off any sentimentality splendidly with an urbanity which is really disarming. After, for example, detailing the closeness of parent and child which is denied him, we can see the rueful shrug:

This, it would seem, was not reserved for me;
Yet this was in my nature; as it is,
I know not what is there, yet something like to this.

III, cxvi

With this ending to the canto we recognise that Byron's poetry has matured; we have the best of travelogue manner; we see a variety of attitudes and responses managed with a flexibility of vocal tones and accents, a fine dramatic voice, and are treated to personal reflection, genuine pathos, melodramatic gestures, idealism, disabusement, gentleness and anger. This is a truly powerful performance, and if we recognise that many of the responses are mutually contradictory we recognise Byron himself, writing passionately and for the moment and taking the reader with him. Sir Walter Scott in his review certainly noticed some difference between this canto and its predecessors and still found it praiseworthy:

> The Third Canto of *Childe Harold* exhibits, in all its strength and in all its peculiarity, the wild, powerful and original vein of poetry which, in the preceding cantos, first fixed the public attention upon the author. If there is any difference, the former seem to us to have been rather more sedulously corrected and revised for publication, and the present work to have been dashed from the author's pen with less regard to the subordinate points of expression and versification. Yet such is the deep and powerful strain of passion, such the original tone and colouring of description, that the want of polish in some of its minute parts rather adds to than deprives the poem of its energy.
>
> CONTEMPORARY REVIEWS OF ROMANTIC POETRY, ed. John Wain

CANTO IV

The long dedicatory letter to Hobhouse not only tells us of the eight years which intervene between the composition of the first and last cantos, referring to the poem as 'the longest, the most thoughtful and comprehensive of my compositions', but dismisses Childe Harold from the poem officially:

> With regard to the conduct of the last canto, there will be found less of the pilgrim than in any of the preceding, and that little

slightly, if at all, separated from the author speaking in his own person.

We are also told the intention of the author in this last canto, namely that Byron intended 'to have touched upon the present state of Italian literature, and perhaps of manner'. And, furthermore, Byron takes the opportunity to express his concern over the state of divided Italy and the insular attitude of England, the supposed mother of freedom, demonstrating himself even more as a citizen of the world, not an Englishman:

> What Italy has gained by the late transfer of nations, it were useless for Englishmen to inquire, till it becomes ascertained that England has acquired something more than a permanent army and a suspended Habeas Corpus; it is enough for them to look at home.

But Byron's concern for Italy is not simply that of the disinterested liberal looking at a bad political situation; he has lost his heart to Italy, and, surprisingly for him, he has been happy in Italy. After only a fortnight in Venice he wrote to his friend Douglas Kinnaird that he had fallen in love with 'a very pretty woman', Marianna Segati, whose marriage was no impediment to the 'incontinent continental system':

> She is not two-and-twenty, with great black eastern eyes, and a variety of subsidiary charms, &c., &c., and amongst her other accomplishments is a mighty and admirable singer—as most of the Italians are—(though not a public one); luckily I can speak the language fluently; and luckily (if I did not), we could employ ourselves a little without talking.
>
> I meant to have given up gallivanting altogether on leaving your country, where I had been tolerably sickened of that and everything else; but, I know how it is, my health growing better, and my spirits not worse, the 'besoin d'aimer' came back upon my heart again, and, after all, there is nothing like it.
>
> LORD BYRON'S CORRESPONDENCE II, 23

The canto opens with a celebration of Venice, a city which fits the overall theme of the poem superlatively, the theme of spoil, time and faded glory, the conquest of men and their works by time and their own folly, the sadness of decay. But it was Rome that fired Byron's imagination and was the inspiration and origin of this final canto. He must have seen this as a possibility for he wrote to Kinnaird four months after the letter just quoted, on 31 March 1817, about his not intending to write for the stage, and he says:

> The drama is complete already; there can be nothing like what has been. You will say this applies to other poetry also; true—but the range is wider, and I look upon the path I struck out in C. Harold as a new one; therefore there can be no comparisons as yet, good or bad. I have done—not much—but enough for me; and having just turned nine-and-twenty, I seriously think of giving up altogether, unless Rome should madden me into a fourth canto, which it may, or may not.
>
> LORD BYRON'S CORRESPONDENCE II, 44

Well, he was maddened when he came to Rome in the late spring, though *maddened* is wholly wrong as a word to describe the temper of this last canto; it is more serene (though without any less of the agony of heart of the third canto) and the tone has deepened, showing a certain resignation in the fate of human life. Sir Walter Scott in a review of the canto in the *Quarterly Review* in April 1818, noted the marked difference between this and the rest of the poem:

> There is less of passion, more of deep thought and sentiment, at once collected and general. The stream which in its earlier course bounds over cataracts and rages through narrow and rocky defiles, deepens, expands, and becomes less turbid as it rolls on, losing the aspect of terror and gaining that of sublimity. Eight years have passed between the appearance of the first volume and the present which concludes the work, a lapse of time which, joined with other circumstances, may have contributed somewhat to moderate the tone of Childe Harold's quarrel with the world, and, if not to reconcile him to his lot, to give him, at least, the firmness which endures it without loud complaint.

He may well be right, but we notice a new note in the opening stanzas, a development of some of the thought of the third canto: we are now presented with the notion of the memory as the key to the survival of glory, and the need of the imagination in order to live adequately in this world:

> The beings of the mind are not of clay;
> Essentially immortal, they create
> And multiply in us a brighter ray
> And more beloved existence: that which Fate
> Prohibits to dull life, in this our state
> Of mortal bondage, by these spirits supplied,
> First exiles, then replaces what we hate;
> Watering the heart whose early flowers have died,
> And with a fresher growth replenishing the void.
>
> IV, *v*

In Canto III we saw the author presenting Harold to himself as a new source of life, now we see the expansion of the faculty of the imagination and its role. Also, in place of the dead heart of Cantos I and II, or the curious situation of Canto III where gloom diminishes with an unnamed loved one, we have the heart whose early flowers have died, but implying a second crop, a regeneration, a resurrection. It is in this new mood that Byron returns throughout this canto to the one thing that seems to survive the fall of empires, the neglect of living poets, the vanity of personal ambitions, the anguish of any individual or nation, and that is literature. What has survived from the ancient civilisation of Italy is the ruin which Byron sees all round him, but also the voices of its long-dead poets, still alive to us, their readers. But, coupled to this, we must recognise that a place is always more than a place, it is meaningful in a mythical sense. It is thus that Venice is seen by the poet. What survives of Venice and its thousand years of glory is twofold: the place itself with its accumulated weight of monuments, and that Venice of the imagination of the poet Byron. So, Byron can say of himself in Stanza ix:

> I twine
> My hopes of being remember'd in my line
> With my land's language:

setting fame in literature as the thing which might outlive time, and perhaps a memory of that famous statement of Horace about being a monument in language more lasting than bronze (*monumentum aere perennius*). And he can say of Venice in Stanza xviii:

> I loved her from my boyhood; she to me
> Was as a fairy city of the heart,
> Rising like water-columns from the sea,
> Of joy the sojourn, and of wealth the mart;
> And Otway, Radcliffe, Schiller, Shakespeare's art,
> Had stamp'd her image in me, . . .

In this frame of mind, and being confronted with his 'green isle of the imagination', he can think of a stoic forbearance, a gritting of the teeth as he now says 'Existence may be borne' and thinks rather less of his own anguish on his journey from Venice to Rome.

On his way he passes the places associated with the famous Italian poets: Arqua with Petrarch, Ferrara with Tasso, Florence with Dante and Ariosto, and he celebrates these great poets, all mistreated while they were alive in one way or another by their cities, and all now the glory of those cities. The analogy is never explicitly drawn between Byron's own situation (or at least the way he sees his own situation) and that of these famous and maltreated poets, but if we were to read on in the canto we would come across Stanza cxxxvi which shows Byron as maltreated by the world (or the equivalent of his 'city'):

> From mighty wrongs to petty perfidy
> Have I not seen what human things could do?
> From the loud roar of foaming calumny
> To the small whisper of the paltry few,
> And subtler venom of the reptile crew,
> The Janus glance of whose significant eye,
> Learning to lie with silence, would *seem* true,
> And without utterance, save the shrug or sigh,
> Deal round to happy fools its speechless obloquy.

But for the moment it seems that the whole country is a constant reminder of *sic transit gloria mundi*, that unvarying theme, and Byron takes a melancholy pleasure in recording that both

Cicero's friend, Servius Sulpicius, and Byron had travelled the same journey in the Aegean. Both had passed the ruins in their respective times of Aegina, Megara, Piraeus and Corinth, and now Byron is seeing the ruins of Servius Sulpicius's Rome:

> all that *was*
> Of then destruction *is*; and now, alas!
> Rome—Rome imperial, bows her to the storm,
> In the same dust and blackness, and we pass
> The skeleton of her Titanic form,
> Wrecks of another world, whose ashes still are warm.

IV, xlvi

It was the idea of destruction, the irony of seeing the same thought about the Greek ruins in a Latin writer as in himself and then seeing more worlds sent to oblivion, rather than any simple aesthetic pleasure in ruins. Byron was never a man to appreciate art in that way; he was never very struck by painting or sculpture, and one of the few things that he records as striking him was the Venus de Medici. Even then he was afraid of simply repeating jargon and had to rest satisfied with indicating its effect upon him; he could not be like 'his connoisseurship' and understand

> The graceful bend, and the voluptuous swell:
> Let these describe the undescribable:
> I would not their vile breath should crisp the stream
> Wherein that image shall for ever dwell.

III, liii

He is more at home 'with Nature rather in the fields,/Than Art in galleries,' and we remember his comments on the paintings he saw of Rubens in Belgium when he set out from England in 1816:

> but as for his works, and his superb 'tableaux', he seems to me (who by the way know nothing of the matter) the most glaring—flaring—staring—harlotry impostor that ever passed a trick upon the senses of mankind,—it is not nature—it is not art—with the exception of some linen (which hangs over the cross in one of his pictures) which, to do it justice, looked like a very handsome

table-cloth—I never saw such an assemblage of florid nightmares as his canvas contains; his portraits seem clothed in pulpit cushions.

LORD BYRON'S CORRESPONDENCE II, 5

Spirited writing, even if, critically, he is the only one in step.

However he was struck by the things about him in Italy, one thing becomes very clear: Byron's meditations in this canto are more an intimate blending of the personal experience of the unique individual Byron and the external world. This is in contradistinction to the loco-descriptive meditation where 'anyman' has the meditation, the poet as spokesman of a culture, a civilisation. It is in opposition too to some of the more Satanic responses we have seen so far in the poem. An example of all this is the way Byron responds to the Italian Apennines. Instead of celebrating them as homes of famous men or deities they are seen as mountains reminding Byron of those more impressive mountains of Greece or the Swiss and Austrian Alps:

> But I have seen the soaring Jungfrau rear
> Her never-trodden snow, and seen the hoar
> Glaciers of bleak Mont Blanc both far and near . . .
>
> IV, *lxxiii*

> . . . And on Parnassus seen the eagles fly
> Like spirits of the spot, as 'twere for fame,
> For still they soared unutterably high:
>
> IV, *lxxiv*

Horace's famous snow-covered Soracte of *Odes* I, 9 starts a private reflection on Byron's memory of being forced to construe Horace at school, and this has destroyed Horace for him as a poet:

> it is a curse
> To understand, not feel thy lyric flow,
> To comprehend, but never love thy verse:

but, Horace apart, Byron celebrates Rome in verse which has not really had its equal in Byron's output. The verse rises to Rome itself as the fount of our civilisation, the 'Niobe of nations':

> Oh Rome! my country! city of my soul!
> The orphans of the world must turn to thee,

> Lone mother of dead empires! and control
> In their shut breasts their petty misery.
> What are our woes and sufferance? Come and see
> The cypress, hear the owl, and plod your way
> O'er steps of broken thrones and temples, Ye!
> Whose agonies are evils of a day—
> A world is at our feet as fragile as our clay.
>
> IV, *lxxviii*

The line of Caesars, the ruined city, the irony of the title of the 'eternal city', all give Byron space to expatiate on his favourite theme, well summed up in Stanzas cviii and cix, especially

> There is the moral of all human tales;
> 'Tis but the same rehearsal of the past,
> First Freedom, and the Glory—when that fails,
> Wealth, vice, corruption,—barbarism at last.
>
> IV, *cviii*

The fountain of Egeria with its legend of the love between an immortal and a man leads Byron into musing on love as an ideal which is unattainable but which 'haunts the unquench'd soul—parch'd, wearied, wrung, and riven' (*cxxi*). As the counterparts to that Romantic notion, we have the twin demons of the phantom luring on the man to destruction, to 'death the sable smoke where vanishes the flame', and the damnation which lies at the heart of life, a doomed and fallen world:

> Our life is a false nature: 'tis not in
> The harmony of things,—this hard decree,
> This uneradicable taint of sin,
> This boundless upas, this all-blasting tree,
> Whose root is earth, whose leaves and branches be
> The skies which rain their plagues on men like dew—
> Disease, death, bondage—all the woes we see,
> And worse, the woes we see not—which throb through
> The immedicable soul, with heart-aches ever new.
>
> IV, *cxxvi*

The superlatives and the despair are essential parts of the statement of this Romantic anguish, but, with resignation, the poet decides not to abandon reason, his 'last and only place of refuge', and to recognise Time as the comforter and restorer, and to respect Nemesis, fate. Here, with a cold anger, he curses his enemies, cursing them with Forgiveness, and ending on a high note of haughty pride, well-known and memorable:

> But I have lived, and have not lived in vain:
> My mind may lose its force, my blood its fire,
> And my frame perish even in conquering pain;
> But there is that within me which shall tire
> Torture and Time, and breathe when I expire;
> Something unearthly, which they deem not of,
> Like the remember'd tone of a mute lyre,
> Shall on their soften'd spirits sink, and move
> In hearts all rocky now the late remorse of love.
>
> IV, *cxxxvii*

In the Coliseum Byron recreates the theatrical death of a Gladiator, one of the many slaughtered for the 'Circus' genial laws,/And the imperial pleasure'. He is one of Byron's best analogues, and, like Byron, he is exiled, separated from his wife and offspring, and dying with his heart far away over the sea in his native land. The analogy is not drawn by the poet, but is felt by the reader, an example of the doctrine of the imagination as so far set out in Cantos III and IV.

After St. Peter's and the Vatican and a stanza (*clxiv*) which brings in the 'Pilgrim', Harold, and dismisses him, we move to Nemi and Albano by the sea. Here Byron comes into his own. The sea has always meant a great deal to him, and one remembers how in Canto III the roar of the sea is one of the turbulent items dismissed for the new transcendent view of nature (III, *lxxv*). The energy of the sea rouses Byron, but its independence of Time and Time's ruins is what engages him now as a resolution of the theme which has run so long in the poem of the conquest of all things by Time. Here is the one permanent, changeless, uncon-querable element, 'the image of eternity, the throne/Of the Invisible'. Shelley thought the address to the sea here one of the peaks of his poetic achievement when he wrote to Byron in 1821 (P. B. Shelley to Byron, 16 April 1821. *Lord Byron's*

Correspondence II, 169), and it certainly is a splendid example of the Byronic rhetoric and eloquence with a boom and inevitability that the very best of Byron in this declamatory sort of poetry has:

> Roll on, thou deep and dark blue Ocean—roll!
> Ten thousand fleets sweep over thee in vain;
> Man marks the earth with ruin—his control
> Stops with the shore; upon the watery plain
> The wrecks are all thy deed, nor doth remain
> A shadow of man's ravage, save his own,
> When, for a moment, like a drop of rain,
> He sinks into thy depths with bubbling groan,
> Without a grave, unknell'd, uncoffin'd, and unknown.
>
> IV, *clxxix*

And with the return to the sea, the personal memories of the boyhood delight and terror in the sea, and the resolution of the major themes of the poem, Byron concludes on a note of the poet's uncertainty about the whole thing, the feeling that it has all been a 'protracted dream'.

Childe Harold's Pilgrimage then is curiously not a unified poem at all if one follows the fictional life of Childe Harold, but a poem which more and more becomes Byron speaking out on a variety of topics in a changing physical situation.

To read through the poem is to witness the failure of Byron's attempt at a Romantic travelogue but the success of finding his own voice.

Much of the verse is ill-suited to the Spenserian stanza, but, at its best, Byron makes of it a good and variable medium for a kaleidoscope of literary effects. It is particularly true of the third and fourth cantos where Byron (and not an author and a Childe Harold competing and confusedly coalescing) sounds out himself, the archetypal suffering Romantic hero, lonely in person and responding to the miseries of the world.

7

Byron as Dramatist

Byron wrote three historical five-act dramas, and one based on a Gothic novel, which should, perhaps, be called a Gothic Drama. His historical dramas are *Marino Faliero, Doge of Venice: An Historical Tragedy in Five Acts*, written in 1820, and *Sardanapalus* and *The Two Foscari*, written in 1821. His Gothic Drama, *Werner*, was written in 1821 and 1822, when he also began but did not finish *The Deformed Transformed*. None of these plays, Byron said, was intended for the stage, and he tried, as far as he could, to forbid and prevent production, not always with success.

All the formal five-act dramas are political plays concerned with the relationship of power, authority, liberty and man's love. All have something of interest, none successful plays; all are exploratory or problem plays, schematic rather than real. *Marino Faliero* can serve as an example.

'MARINO FALIERO'

In the careful introduction to this play Byron sets out the historical facts of the case and offers what seem to be weighty reasons for the apparent rebellion of a head of state against the state, and he shows how much the story interested him. But, equally importantly, he sets out the case for the non-performance of his play. The stage in England is in a poor way; he would think it far too painful to fail on the stage and success would give him no pleasure. His sentences have a very 18th-century ring to them:

> The sneering reader, and the loud critic, and the tart review, are scattered and distant calumnies; but the trampling of an intelligent

or of an ignorant audience on a production which, be it good or bad, has been a mental labour to the writer, is a palpable and immediate grievance, heightened by a man's doubt of their competency to judge, and his certainty of his own imprudence in electing them his judges.

The play presents a fiery old man, full of years and a high honour, whose very honour has been publicly insulted in the person of his young wife, who learns that the judgment on the insulter, Steno, is simply a month's imprisonment. Nothing less than death would have satisfied Marino Faliero and he meditates revenge against the state itself, the patricians. Though he is Doge of Venice and titular head of state, he has no real power; this makes it possible for Byron to treat the historical story under the general rubric of 'tyranny' and see it as meaningful in terms of his own time's political struggles.

The notion of freedom is brought in by making it plain that the 'patricians' are mishandling affairs in the state and there is consequent discontent amongst the lower orders. An old soldier, a state servant, a former veteran under the Doge, comes to him to claim redress against a patrician who struck him in the course of his state duty. His major purpose is to sound out the Doge to lead a rebellion which is brewing up, and to persuade him that the whole city-state is in a ferment, and in this he is highly successful.

The second act presents Marino Faliero and his young wife, Angiolina. She is allowed a conversation with a friend to show her sincere love for her husband and her scorn of the insult which has so incensed the Doge. The Doge and Angiolina together bring out their reasons for their marriage and the good that exists on both their sides, the Doge, incidentally, uttering several trenchant thoughts about love, lust and romantic love;

> For love, romantic love, which in my youth
> I knew to be illusion, and ne'er saw
> Lasting, but often fatal, it had been
> No lure for me, in my most passionate days,
> And could not be so now, did such exist.

II, i, 349–53

This is reflection enough on the Romantic hero and his loves, but the old-fashioned side of Byron, which was always there, comes out in the Doge's view of fallen woman:

> The once fall'n woman must for ever fall;
> For vice must have variety, while virtue
> Stands like the sun, and all which rolls around
> Drinks life, and light, and glory from her aspect.
>
> II, 395-8

In the next scene, two of the leaders of the rebellion, Israel Bertuccio (who had complained to the Doge) and Philip Calendaro, discuss one of their members, Bertram. It is this man who is to be the cause of the failure of the rebellion by warning his patrician friend of his death if he goes out of doors. The irony is that he has a good heart, but it is this good heart which brings destruction on the Doge and his followers, and praise is given to the sort of person that he is. Byron, himself, was often gentle and very disturbed by slaughter and bloodshed, and the reader sees Byron perhaps warning himself in the context of Italian rebellions. Bertram certainly has a soft heart but this must be recognised as more than gentleness because

>   there exists
> Oft in concentred spirits not less daring
> Than in more loud avengers.
>
> II, ii, 64-6

and

> The truly brave are soft of heart and eyes,
> And feel for what their duty bids them do.
>
> II, ii, 74-5

The Doge is seen, too, to have characteristics of the Byronic hero: he is aristocratic, haughty, proud, courageous and readily roused,

> And add too, that his mind is liberal,
> He sees and feels the people are oppress'd
> And shares their sufferings.
>
> II, ii, 174-6

Just like Byron in Italy.

Act III opens with the symbolic situation of the 'Space between the Canal and the Church of San Giovanni e San Paolo. An equestrian Statue before it'. Marino Faliero himself stands in the space between his old life as the Doge and his new life as a leader of the rabble against the state he has for so many years served so well and faithfully. His ancestors are buried in the church nearby; he is both near his sum of years and his death as a traitor, viewed in terms of the play and of history. He is poised between worlds, and this is perhaps the best dramatic moment in all of Byron's work, a really compelling situation if visualised and seen in its forceful symbolism. The speech rises to the occasion and the Doge has some splendid rhetoric:

> Tall fane!
> Where sleep my fathers, whose dim statues shadow
> The floor which doth divide us from the dead,
> Where all the pregnant hearts of our bold blood,
> Moulder'd into a mite of ashes, hold
> In one shrunk heap what once made many heroes,
> When what is now a handful shook the earth—
>
> III, i, 15–21

As in *Childe Harold's Pilgrimage* IV, there is a preoccupation with dimness, death, the little dust that remains of greatness, and yet the greatness that was possible. One of the ironies is that Marino Faliero is himself shrunk in age and is near to death, and that *his* greatness, too, lies in his glorious deeds of the past, like his conquest of the Turk at Zara. Again, ironically, Marino Faliero invokes Odelafo, his ancestor who died at Zara where he had conquered (and he is now to be conquered in his turn).

There is irony again when he is talking to Israel Bertuccio about the future if their attempt succeeds. We know the outcome from history:

> If this
> Attempt succeeds, and Venice render'd free
> And flourishing, when we are in our graves,
> Conducts her generations to our tombs,
> And makes her children with their little hands

Strew flowers o'er her deliverers' ashes, then
The consequence will sanctify the deed,
And we shall be like the two Bruti in
The annals of hereafter.

III, i, 67–75

The whole of the action of this powerful scene is dominated
by the equestrian statue, a

> tall warrior's statue
> Bestriding a proud steed, in the dim light
> Of the dull moon.

III, i, 86–8

and this anonymous protector seems menacing the little men
down below who are trying to overthrow a state with such
magnificence of martial splendour and achievement behind it.
He was, again ironically, the ancestor of the Doge, now the last
of his line, and he feels the disturbance in his ancestors looking
down on his rebellion:

> Deem'st thou the souls of such a race as mine
> Can rest, when he, their last descendant chief,
> Stands plotting on the brink of their pure graves
> With stung plebians?

III, i, 99–102

The Doge puts himself into the category of men like Bertram
who cannot act without feeling:

> No—but I *feel*, and shall do to the last.
> I cannot quench a glorious life at once
> Nor dwindle to the thing I now must be,
> And take men's lives by stealth, without some pause . . .

III, i, 105–8

The next scene of the meeting of the conspirators continues
the developing thematic relationship of Bertram and the Doge.
Bertram is made to stand against the levelling fury of his fellow
conspirators by his 'softness', but he is roused 'like yourselves to
overthrow oppression', though he claims to be

93

A kind man, I am apt to think, as some
Of you have found me; and if brave or no,
You, Calendaro, can pronounce, who have seen me
Put to the proof; or, if you should have doubts,
I'll clear them on your person!

III, ii, 53–7

He has, as one thinks, Byron's hatred of blood spilt in war:

                    the sight
Of blood which spouts through hoary scalps is not
To me a thing of triumph, nor the death
Of men surprised a glory.

III, ii, 66–9

On the other hand, the Doge, when he comes on the scene, shows himself a fierce old warrior who cannot bring himself *really* to think of himself as a leader of the rebellious rabble, and it slips out in his speech:

I cannot stoop—that is, I am not fit
To lead a band of—patriots . . .

III, ii, 220–1

He remembers all the patricians as his former friends or comrades, but now they have fallen from him

As faithless leaves drop from the o'erblown flower,
All left me a lone blighted thorny stalk,
Which, in its solitude, can shelter nothing;
So, as they let me wither, let them perish.

III, ii, 309–12

This thought remains with him and nags him in conversation with Israel Bertuccio after the other conspirators have left; he feels that he is not even acting freely:

And yet I act no more on my free will,
Nor my own feelings—both compel me back;
But there is *hell* within me and around,
And like the demon who believes and trembles
Must I abhor and do.

III, ii, 517–21

Again, the play associates Bertram and the Doge, when Israel Bertuccio calls the Doge's state of heart a 'strange compunction'.

The irony of this 'strange compunction' comes home when, in Act IV Scene i, we see Bertram try to warn his friend and benefactor, Lioni the Patrician, which will mean the discovery and eventual miscarriage of the rebellion. But before Bertram enters, Lioni has a long soliloquy presaging dire events and yet managing to be a meditation on the waste of time, energy and beauty that goes into all-night revels, a sort of post-revel Byron musing, admiring both women at the ball and Venice in the moonlight:

> The many-twinkling feet so small and sylph-like,
> Suggesting the more secret symmetry
> Of the fair forms which terminate so well . . .
>
> IV, *i*, 59–61

and

>   the dash
> Phosphoric of the oar, or rapid twinkle
> Of the far lights of skimming gondolas,
> And the responsive voices of the choir
> Of boatmen answering back with verse for verse.
>
> IV, *i*, 96–100

And so, for a moment, another side of Byron is let loose in the play, though one can say that the soliloquy suggests a permanent Venice which lies behind all the politics, a Venice which was essentially the same in Byron's time, that Venice of love and moonlight. But the play will not allow this interlude to be more than an ironic placing of one view of Venice against the other of a city-state enduring a sort of tyranny. When the Doge is arrested the next scene closes with the foiled plot, and his speech ends with the message for the Venice of Byron's own time:

> They cannot quench the memory of those
> Who would have hurl'd them from their guilty thrones,
> And such examples will find heirs, though distant.
>
> IV, *ii*, 312–14

Act V shows the separated Angiolina and allows her an

opportunity to draw moral lessons from the consequences of her husband's sense of honour. Despite the fact that he is now under sentence of death and in disgrace, the moral lesson is not about abating pride, or using more common sense, or attempting to curb the disposition to high-flown and terrible anger, but, rather, a lesson

> To wretches how they tamper in their spleen
> With beings of a higher order.

V, i, 433–4

No better way could there be of showing where Byron's aristocratic sympathies lie, and the reasons why this story should so appeal to the English milord involved in fostering and sustaining revolution in Italy.

Byron's sympathies come out in the interview between the Doge and his wife. There the Doge says, curiously, that

> there was that in my spirit ever
> Which shaped out for itself some great reverse;
> The marvel is, it came not until now—
> And yet it was foretold me.

V, ii, 11–14

Byron's superstitious nature is at work again, and the Doge tells of the prophecy of the Bishop whom he struck down while he was carrying the sacred Host, the 'unwonted density' of mist when he first landed in Venice as Doge making him disembark between the pillars of Saint Mark's, where criminals were put to death, instead of at the Riva della Paglia, and his belief in Fate and in the men who condemned him as instruments 'of an o'erruling power'. Enough, even for Byron.

The final tragic irony of the play is the beheading of the Doge at the place where he was crowned, and the play ends with a terrible prophecy (indictment) of Venice as a future (present) sink of slavery and viciousness:

> Vice without splendour, sin without relief
> Even from the gloss of love to smooth it o'er,
> But in its stead, coarse lusts of habitude,

> Prurient yet passionless, cold studied lewdness,
> Depraving nature's frailty to an art . . .

V, iii, 85–9

Though, dramatically, there are weak things in this play, nevertheless it is Byron's best play and has a masterly handling of the irony of the situations, with a very skilful use of the central scene and its multiple ironies. His language certainly owes something to Shakespeare, but it is not derivative Shakespearean drama. It is of Byron's own time and he has well handled the historical material to make both a play of dramatic interest and a sounding out of his notions of freedom and the part of the aristocracy which must be played, albeit difficult, and entailing outlawry and the cutting of ties with the past.

'THE TWO FOSCARI'

This play of 1821 is a Venetian play, as was *Marino Faliero*, again centred around the Doge. This time the Doge's last remaining son has returned illicitly from exile, and after torture is again condemned to exile, but he dies as a result of the torture, and another noble line is extinct. That, basically, is the story, and resemblance between the two Venetian plays is frequent. The themes of the play are the exploration of the concept of the State, the definition of loyalty, the notion of tyranny and the relationship of compassion to ruthlessness in political life. But, though the play is too slight for a full five-act drama, Byron has managed very well to convey a whole spectrum of attitudes to the State and one's responsibility and role within it, and the play does display them clearly. But dramatically they do not work one against another, and we have a feeling of being offered several concurrent stories which only exist because of the ideas. Types are set together simply for the attitude or idea they convey.

'SARDANAPALUS'

Of the same date as *The Two Foscari*, *Sardanapalus* is essentially a bipartite play; in the first part we have a luxury-loving and easy-going monarch of a great state who finds that he is going to be involved in a rebellion, and the second part shows his being aroused and fighting like a tiger to the very end and then committing suicide with his slave-lover.

In the very first scene of the play the warrior, Salemenes, the abandoned queen's brother, indicates the unrest in the state and shows up the basic paradox in Sardanapalus's make-up:

> In his effeminate heart
> There is a careless courage which corruption
> Has not all quench'd, and latent energies,
> Repress'd by circumstance, but not destroy'd—

I, i, 9–12

No Byronic hero can be as bad as he might be painted. Byron surrounded himself with ostentatiously impressive beds and gewgaws and yet could live with a spartan simplicity; a pointer to Sardanapalus as Byron conceives him.

It is hard to know exactly what this play is about; it is a love story (but not of ordinary lovers), a war story, a display of the relation of pacifism to the real political needs of a state, the demonstration of the two sides of a man of heroic stature who is pleasure-loving and murder-hating, and yet courageous and fearless in battle.

Sardanapalus is a sympathetic character who is gentle in his treatment of others, who tries to see life as something to be richly enjoyed, and who has the gift of reading hearts with compassion and understanding. His complementary woman, Myrrha, the Greek slave, is an active masculine-minded woman, and we are led into thinking partly of Macbeth and Lady Macbeth and partly into Byron's biography.

Many themes concerning human political activity and man's necessary involvement in bloodshed for the defence of a cause in which he believes are forcefully presented in this play because these were the thoughts that Byron himself was undergoing, and from this involvement the play, at times, catches fire. There is more dramatic interest in this play, and there is a sense of development in the hero, and Myrrha acts as foil and counterweight to Sardanapalus to increase the range of the play, to raise it from a personal story to a more universal one.

This is Byron's last completed play, written between 1821 and 1822, and dedicated to Goethe. He says in the preface that he had been working on the first act of a play in 1815 which was adapted from a Gothic tale, *German's Tale, Kruitzner*, which he had read as a boy. This play follows the same tale, one that made a big impression on him, 'and may indeed, be said to contain the germ of much that I have written ever since'.

Perhaps it is lucky that not all of his work was impregnated by the *German's Tale*, as this play is an extraordinary piece of work, a truly Gothic play. There are ruined castles, secret panels, midnight slaughters, banditti, aristocratic opulence and display, sudden leaps to fortune, mysterious entanglements of relationship, a son lost and found, a hero-figure much too large for life (with that Byronic attractiveness about him that none can resist), the reversal of the reader's belief about who is guilty of the murder, and so on.

Apart from the tedious melodrama there are one or two things that might be said in the play's favour; it is a play about guilt, especially inherited guilt (and such would have impressed a younger Byron with *his* ancestry). It is also a play about the two sides of a person, a little like *Sardanapalus*; where the father abhors killing, the son is a cruel and cold-blooded murderer. As the father, Siegendorf, says:

> *My* son! *mine*! who have ever
> Abhorr'd both mystery and blood, and yet
> Am plunged into the deepest hell of both!
>
> V, *i*, 480–2

And, perhaps, one ought to make a point a little more strongly that there is often an energy in the verse of this play which one might think wasted on such melodrama. One has to praise, for example, a sort of Elizabethan pastiche, if only as pastiche, in the response of the steward, Idenstein, to the sight of a diamond ring with which he is being bribed. Memories of Ben Jonson jostle with Shakespeare's *Henry IV, ii* (III, *i*) and *Henry V* (IV, *i*).

Oh, thou sweet sparkler!
Thou more than stone of the philosopher!
Thou touchstone of Philosophy herself!
Thou bright eye of the Mine! thou loadstar of
The Soul! the true magnetic Pole to which
All hearts point duly north, like trembling needles!
Thou flaming Spirit of the Earth! which, sitting
High on the monarch's diadem, attractest
More worship than the majesty who sweats
Beneath the crown which makes his head ache, like
Millions of hearts which bleed to lend it lustre!

III, *i*, 328–38

But, when all this is said, there seems not to be a very great play before us in *Werner*.

'THE DEFORMED TRANSFORMED'

This uncompleted play, written in 1822, can be seen as a transition between the 'Mystery' play and the Drama proper in the work of Byron's maturity.

Again, Byron's work was based on a sort of fact, this time on literary facts, the novel *The Three Brothers* and Goethe's *Faust*. The story is simple enough: a hunchback is visited by the Devil who gives him a splendid body and takes his own for himself. They set out, rather like Don Quixote and Sancho Panza, for adventures of a mostly military kind and take part in the siege and capture of Rome.

Part I scene i opens with a mother upbraiding her son for his hunchback deformity, and here we remember Byron's reaction to his own mother and see the contribution autobiography plays here too, though Arnold seems most unByronically long-suffering and meek. His solution is to attempt suicide, but just as he is about to fall on his dagger a 'tall black man' appears theatrically from a cloud of mist and a fountain. He speaks with an assurance and *savoir-faire* that bespeak 'the devil', suave, witty and disdainful (more like one part of Byron himself).

Though deformed, Arnold claims to have an 'aspiring soul'

when the stranger is offering to give him a new body of whatever sort he chooses. He also, when he has made his choice of body, does not want to ask for valour 'since deformity is daring':

> It is its essence to o'ertake mankind
> By heart and soul, and make itself the equal—
> Ay, the superior of the rest. There is
> A spur in its halt movements, to become
> All that the others cannot, in such things
> As still are free to both, to compensate
> For stepdame Nature's avarice at first.
> They woo with fearless deeds and smiles of fortune,
> And oft, like Timour the lame Tartar, win them.
>
> I, i, 315–23

This is Byron's apologia, as we can see from the choice of 'halt movement' and 'Timour the lame Tartar', and it certainly is the best expression of the psychological spur which often guided Byron's own activities in all sorts of fields, mental and physical, his pride in playing cricket for Harrow, his pistol-shooting, his feats of swimming and so on.

The stranger takes Arnold's shape, with wit nonetheless (and he is going to call himself 'Caesar' into the bargain); he is black but

> I might be whiter; but I have a penchant
> For black—it is so honest, and besides
> Can neither blush with shame nor pale with fear . . .
>
> I, i, 373–5

Arnold wants some action and wants to go 'where the world/Is thickest'; the stranger replies, almost like Byron in a letter:

> That's to say, where there is war
> And woman in activity. Let's see!
> Spain—Italy—the new Atlantic World—
> Afric, with all its Moors. In very truth,
> There is small choice: the whole race are just now
> Tugging as usual at each others' hearts.
>
> I, i, 496–501

But off they go to Rome, and the next scene shows Arnold obviously highly successful in war, and most unhappy because he wants peace. It is the stranger, now Caesar, who has the best talk in the play and here he has a fine speech on life as motion and nothing else:

> From the star
> To the winding worm, all life is motion; and
> In life *commotion* is the extremest point
> Of life. The planet wheels till it becomes
> A comet, and destroying as it sweeps
> The stars, goes out. The poor worm winds its way,
> Living upon the death of other things,
> But still, like them, must live and die, the subject
> Of something which has made it live and die.
>
> I, *ii*, 22–30

Here Caesar takes up Cain's speech to Lucifer in *Cain* II: on the order in the universe and gives an answer in terms of 'necessity' and not anything divine. All is fixed eternally.

They take part in the siege, attack and sack of Rome, and Arnold is seen to be a brave leader of men, while Caesar is sardonic, mocking, and a witty commentator on all things human. Some parts are very good in a callous sort of way, like the retort Caesar makes to Arnold when he has said that he will not be Arnold's rival for the affections of the lady who could obviously become the heroine if the play were to continue:

> I could be one right formidable;
> But since I slew the seven husbands of
> Tobias' future bride (and after all
> Was smoked out by some incense), I have laid
> Aside intrigue: 'tis rarely worth the trouble
> Of gaining, or—what is more difficult—
> Getting rid of your prize again; for there's
> The rub! at least to mortals.
>
> II, *ii*, 179–86

Byron's very tone and accents in his mankind-mocking mood.

The interest of this little play is simply that Byron was writing

Don Juan simultaneously, and we can see the same basic situation of a naïve and gentlemanly hero accompanied by the sardonic commentator on human life and affairs, though in *Don Juan* the commentator is at your elbow and is not, strictly speaking, an embodied character, not even in a borrowed body.

8

Satanic Melodrama: 'Manfred' and 'Cain'

There are a number of works in which Byron attempted to present and work out his preoccupations with central questions about man's life, his freedom or his compulsion by Fate, his guilt, merited or preordained, and the whole set of philosophical questions which disturbed him to a greater or less extent all his life.

The most important of these, and the earliest, is *Manfred*, written in 1816. It is subtitled, 'A Dramatic Poem', but it is really an internal struggle exteriorised, rather than a dramatic play: we are really concerned with the mind of one man, and he does not seem to be a man at all, but Byronic Romanticism personified. If we say that a Faust-like figure conjures up mighty spirits in order to discover hidden arcana and that this is really only a Romantic bit of the Faust legend, we must remember that the spirits are really the creations of the mind. This means that we have more of a situation where we are being asked to look at the relation between the Imagination and its imaginings, or the Author and his works. It turns out to be the old relation of Idealism as seen in respect of the reality of the body and its passions.

There is no denying that this is a strange work, and many things were at work in the background of the poem which ought to be briefly mentioned. There were the personal emotional, moral and philosophical difficulties that Byron was experiencing as a result of his incestuous relationship with his half-sister Augusta; this involved remorse, a feeling of damnation and a questioning of the whole meaning of this life. There was also Byron's brief introduction to Goethe's *Faust*, parts of which

'Monk' Lewis read to him in 1816 in translation, as Byron knew no German. And, extremely importantly, there were the discussions with Shelley which were talks about 'metaphysics', and both men were impressive talkers. Other parts of the background are complex, but one ought to mention Aeschylus's work and the whole range of Gothic horror, so much of a vogue in England, and so deeply impressed on Byron's young imagination.

So the poem opens in a Gothic enough manner:

> Manfred alone—Scene, a Gothic Gallery.—Time Midnight.

But it is not Faust that we meet when the curtain rises, but a man of satiety, full of a too-complete human experience, with no emotion left. (We are among friends . . .)

> Good, or evil, life,
> Powers, passions, all I see in other beings,
> Have been to me as rain unto the sands,
> Since that all-nameless hour. I have no dread,
> And feel the curse to have no natural fear,
> Nor fluttering throb, that beats with hopes or wishes,
> Or lurking love of something on the earth.
>
> I, i, 21–7

What is demanded of the seven spirits that Manfred conjures up is not Faustian at all; he wants 'forgetfulness' and 'oblivion, self-oblivion'. His attitude to these spirits (and to everything) is one of savage pride in himself, an unholy Satanism:

> Slaves, scoff not at my will!
> The mind, the spirit, the Promethean spark,
> The lightning of my being, is as bright,
> Pervading, and far darting as your own,
> And shall not yield to yours, though coop'd in clay!
>
> I, i, 153–7

As a true Byronic figure Manfred wants nothing earthly, no 'Kingdom, and sway, and strength, and length of days—', but he hungers for the unearthly beauty which might exist, and 'ere we part,/I would behold ye face to face'. Now, rather like Dr. Faustus and Helen, a spirit appears 'in the shape of a beautiful female figure' whom Manfred tries to embrace. She vanishes and he falls senseless, moaning 'My heart is crush'd'. While he is senseless we hear a lyrical incantation (sounding rather like the interspersed lyrics in the 'dramas' of Byron's contemporary Thomas Lovell Beddoes but whose major work was not published until 1850). This was originally written separately as a curse upon Byron's wife, and was one of the pieces most praised by Shelley, but as we have it now it is Manfred who is destined to damnation in the orthodox Byronic manner. The 'star' which rules Manfred's destiny used to be as a world 'fresh and fair', but has become

> A wandering mass of shapeless flame,
> A pathless comet, and a curse,
> The menace of the universe:

> I, *i*, 117–19

as the Seventh Spirit announced previously. Now we are told more specifically that

> a magic voice and verse
> Hath baptized thee with a curse;
> And a spirit of the air
> Hath begirt thee with a snare;
> In the wind there is a voice
> Shall forbid thee to rejoice;

> I, *i*, 222–7

but then we are told that Manfred is evil and has brought all this upon himself. Here is where the conflict between the original curse as written for his wife betrays Byron into inconsistency. It does look as though his wife, in Byron's eyes, ought to have heard the hiss of:

> By thy cold breast and serpent smile,
> By thy unfathom'd gulfs of guile,
> By that most seeming virtuous eye,
> By thy shut soul's hypocrisy;
> By the perfection of thine art
> Which pass'd for human thine own heart;

By thy delight in others' pain,
And by thy brotherhood of Cain,
I call upon thee! and compel
Thyself to be thy proper Hell!

I, i, 242–51

In the following scene with Manfred alone on the Jungfrau we
listen to one of the aspects of the Romantic agony; Manfred can
see but cannot love the beauty of Nature. We are reminded of
Coleridge's despairing cry of

I see them all so excellently fair,
I see, not feel, how beautiful they are!

DEJECTION: An Ode, II, 37–8

when Manfred says:

Why are ye beautiful? I cannot love ye.

I, ii, 9

Manfred seems to combine elements of Hamlet's speech in II, ii
on the supposed qualities of man, Hamlet's notion of an overall
purpose in life which we men cannot avoid ('There's a divinity
that shapes our ends,/Rough-hew them how we will'), and
Pope's splendid exhibition of the paradox of man, 'The glory,
jest, and riddle of the world!' at the opening of Epistle II of
the *Essay on Man*.

We hear all the echoes in:

How beautiful is all this visible world!
How glorious in its action and itself!
But we, who name ourselves its sovereigns, we,
Half dust, half deity, alike unfit
To sink or soar . . .

I, ii, 37–41

Verbally Manfred reminds us of Hamlet's supposed adulation of
man ('what a piece of work is a man . . . the beauty of the world'
. . .) but Manfred is concerned with the world and its beauty and
not man and his faculties, though we ought to remember *Hamlet*
when reading *Manfred* as there are many relationships there.

107

As he is about to throw himself from the rocks Manfred is rescued by a Chamois Hunter, and Act II opens in his cottage in the Alps. There we come to see that Manfred is suffering, among other things, from a secret and dreadful sin, Romantic enough to allow us to murmur 'incest'. Manfred, on being offered a cup of wine sees blood on the rim, and this fantasy draws out the guilty sin:

> When we were in our youth, and had one heart,
> And loved each other as we should not love,
> And this was shed:
>
> II, i, 26–8

The Chamois Hunter speaks wiser than he knows when he calls this 'some half-maddening sin', and says that all this sort of thing is 'convulsion, and no healthful life'. But Manfred doesn't live by the same rules as others; his time is *intensity* (as it should be for a Romantic poet) and his life is a desert:

> but actions are our epochs: mine
> Have made my days and nights imperishable,
> Endless, and all alike, as sands on the shore,
> Innumerable atoms; and one desert,
> Barren and cold, on which the wild waves break,
> But nothing rests, save carcasses and wrecks,
> Rocks, and the salt-surf weeds of bitterness.
>
> II, i, 52–58

And, of course, such barrenness of soul is linked, as we should by now expect, with a fatal love which brings destruction on those who loved him:

> My injuries come down on those who loved me—
> On those whom I best loved: I never quell'd
> An enemy, save in my just defence—
> But my embrace was fatal.
>
> II, i, 84–7

The fatality is also indicated by the Witch of the Alps whom Manfred conjures up in the next scene; she tells him that

I know thee for a man of many thoughts,
And deeds of good and ill, extreme in both,
Fatal and fated in thy sufferings.

II, ii, 34–6

Manfred gives her and us a long *apologia pro vita sua* explaining his childhood exultation in his solitary enjoyment of Nature in her extremes of 'The difficult air of the iced mountain's top' and his love to

plunge

Into the torrent, and to roll along
On the swift whirl of the new breaking wave
Of river-stream, or ocean. . . .

II, ii, 65–8

He lived as apart from men as he could, and spent time in studying arcana, 'sciences untaught,/Save in the old time', and with his knowledge grew the thirst of knowledge. All this seems a curious combination of the Renaissance thirst for knowledge, so amply displayed by Marlowe, for instance, and the Romantic melancholy, but the Romantic dominates for he had a loved one who could not but be Romantic. She was a mirror-image of himself:

She was like me in lineaments; her eyes,
Her hair, her features, all, to the very tone
Even of her voice, they said were like to mine;
But soften'd all, and temper'd into beauty:

II, ii, 105–8

This might well have been Byron's idealised portrait of Augusta, but the woman Manfred loved is intellectually his equal with 'the same lone thoughts and wanderings', which could not be said of Augusta. But, inevitably, the woman was destroyed:

Not with my hand, but heart, which broke her heart;
It gazed on mine, and wither'd.

II, ii, 117–18

This destruction has so preyed on Manfred's mind that he has tried all ways that he can think of to find forgetfulness, but all

109

to no avail. He has even, like Byron in *Childe Harold's Pilgrimage* III and IV, tried imaginative writing:

> In fantasy, imagination, all
> The affluence of my soul—which one day was
> A Croesus in creation—I plunged deep,
> But, like an ebbing wave, it dash'd me back
> Into the gulf of my unfathom'd thought.

II, *ii*, 140–4

And so autobiography and creative work seem inextricably mixed in Byron and it grows hard to separate one strand from another, if not simply impossible.

A true hero, Manfred refuses to swear obedience to the Witch's will, and then decides to call up the dead, lamenting his loved one's present predicament again:

> What is she now?—a sufferer for my sins—
> A thing I dare not think upon—or nothing.

II, *ii*, 196–7

Act II Scene iii is a Byronic version of the Three Weird Sisters in *Macbeth*, but with Manfred as the tragic hero whose life is being controlled by Destiny (or Nemesis—Byron's favourite word). Where the *Macbeth* play had had Hecate as the superintendent goddess, Byron has Nemesis, but this time we are in the 19th century and much of the talk is about tyranny and freedom. Of course, the Destinies are on the side of destruction of man and destruction of freedom, but Byron shows that his heart is in the right place by allowing Nemesis to state the possibility of the destruction of the old tyrannies; people are starting to 'ponder for themselves' and think of 'freedom, the forbidden fruit'.

The final scene of the second act sees us inside the realm of 'evil', the Hall of Arimanes, who seems to stand for the other power which shares the ruling of the universe with God, the equivalent of Satan, but with more power. He has power over destruction, chaos, tempest, earthquakes, volcanoes, pestilence, war, death, 'life with all its infinite of agonies', and seems powerful enough in all conscience. Manfred enters and, true to form, does not bow down and adore; on the contrary, he is quite willing to go down on his knees provided that Arimanes will do so too and adore

> The overruling Infinite—the Maker
> Who made him not for worship—
>
> II, iv, 47–8

This sort of reply angers the Destinies, though the First Destiny thinks Manfred highly commendable; he is no common man:

> his sufferings
> Have been of an immortal nature, like
> Our own;
>
> II, iv, 53–5

and

> his aspirations
> Have been beyond the dwellers of the earth,
> And they have only taught him what we know—
> That knowledge is not happiness, and science
> But an exchange of ignorance for that
> Which is another kind of ignorance.
>
> II, iv, 58–63

We can see that a bond of sympathy is strung like a halter between Manfred and the spirit world, and as Another Spirit says:

> Had he been one of us, he would have made
> An awful spirit.
>
> II, iv, 162–3

Manfred calls up 'Astarte', his loved one, and has an agony of conscience:

> Thou lovedst me
> Too much, as I loved thee: we were not made
> To torture thus each other, though it were
> The deadliest sin to love as we have loved.
>
> II, iv, 121–4

But he learns very little from her, apart from predicting that he will die the following day, and she says little that could be construed as encouraging or consoling him.

The scene is therefore set for the climax of the play, the announced and predicted death of Manfred; what more could there possibly be, as we have been through the realm of spirits and learnt as much as we could from them about life and its meaning. In Act III Scene i Manfred has a talk with an Abbot who comes to bring him back to penitence and reconcilement with the Church. Manfred draws himself up to his full height (about the same as Milton's Satan) and tells the Abbot what he thinks of all that:

> Old man! there is no power in holy men,
> Nor charm in prayer, nor purifying form
> Of penitence, nor outward look, nor fast,
> Nor agony—nor, greater than all these,
> The innate tortures of that deep despair,
> Which is remorse without the fear of hell,
> But all in all sufficient to itself
> Would make a hell of heaven—can exorcise
> From out the unbounded spirit the quick sense
> Of its own sins, wrongs, sufferance, and revenge
> Upon itself; there is no future pang
> Can deal that justice on the self-condemn'd
> He deals on his own soul.
>
> III, _i_, 66–78

This damnable pride of the 'self-condemn'd' goes hand in hand with what Manfred has to say about his early aspirations of serving mankind; he did so want to do good to men until he discovered the ways that he should have to behave, and then he would have none of it. He should have to 'serve' and 'soothe and sue' and 'be a living lie' in order to become

> A mighty thing amongst the mean, and such
> The mass are; I disdain'd to mingle with
> A herd, though to be a leader—and of wolves.
> The lion is alone, and so am I.
>
> III, _i_, 120–3

We are meant to be impressed by this, though in our egalitarian time it plays an odd tune, but the Abbot is obviously impressed by the wasted potential he sees in Count Manfred.

In the next scene we are drawing closer to the end, as we know from the place and time; we are in Manfred's chamber and the sun is setting. This occasion allows Byron to pull out his *vox humana* and sing splendidly about the sun and its power and glory. The verse is artificial and exclamatory, but a fine rhetorical set-piece of thirty lines or so.

Scene three shows us Manfred's retainers giving us some of the 'mysterious' background to Manfred's life and activities. Strange things have been known to have gone on in the Tower, no one knows what exactly, but Astarte was there too. The Abbot enters to try his hand at redemption again, and he will be in at the death in the following scene, marking out an essential difference between Marlowe's *Dr. Faustus* and *Manfred*.

The final scene, the death scene, opens with Manfred still doing his fine rhetoric, now on Night and the Coliseum. Childe Harold has come home to roost, but without the twin salvations of his redemptive love and his calm accepting of the inevitable destruction of all things by time.

When the Abbot reappears there is nothing further that can be done. Manfred's time is up. Instead of howling magnificently like Dr. Faustus, or submitting to his recovering demon with aplomb, he defies the spirits who come for him, even though he knows that defiance or any other attitude will avail him nothing:

> I stand
> Upon my strength—I do defy—deny—
> Spurn back, and scorn ye!
>
> III, *iv*, 119–21

He is proud, self-condemned Manfred to the end:

> I bear within
> A torture which could nothing gain from thine:
> The mind which is immortal makes itself
> Requital for its good or evil thoughts,—

> Is its own origin of ill and end—
> And its own place and time:

III, *iv*, 127–32

And, with an eerily quiet 'Old man! 'tis not so difficult to die' another indomitable mind comes to its inevitable doom.

John Wilson, reviewing *Manfred* in *Blackwood's* in June 1817, shows how the poem appealed to something which Byron touched in the contemporary reader, the feeling that revelations about the human soul were being made to people who could only know these terrible things dimly:

> There are in his poetry feelings, thoughts, sentiments, and passions, that we at once recognise to be human though we know not whence they come: they break upon us like the sudden flash of a returning dream—like some wild cry from another world. And even those whose lives have had little experience of the wilder passions, for a moment feel that an unknown region of their own souls has been revealed to them, and that there are indeed fearful mysteries in our human nature.

Many of us now would doubt that it reveals universally true human situations or values, though we can appreciate the passionate expression of a lot of Byron's own thoughts about his own situation. Wilson perhaps comes nearer to something that we in our century can appreciate just as well as his, and that is the influence of the mountains on the poem:

> But though . . . it is difficult to comprehend distinctly the drift of the composition, and almost impossible to give any thing like a distinct account of it, it unquestionably exhibits many noble delineations of mountain scenery—many impressive and terrible pictures of passion—and many wild and awful visions of imagery and horror.

We should not choose his words, so intimately involved with Romanticism, but we should have to agree with what he is saying.

But we should want to say, too, that Manfred is one of the family of doomed heroes, misanthropically spurning mankind, incestuously involved and blighted. This time 'metaphysics' has reared its head, though the spirits are not like those of Shelley, having an independent existence in Mind, but are firmly related to a specific mind, Manfred's, the type of the Romantic rebel and poet. This is the wildest of the Satanic melodramas, and perhaps the best even if the thought is muddled, silly or contradictory at times.

'CAIN: A MYSTERY'

Byron said, in a fragment of a surviving letter to Hobhouse, postmarked 16 October 1821, that he had sent to Murray 'A "Manfred" sort of thing called "Cain".' (*Lord Byron's Correspondence* II, 202)

This is a three-act drama worked out around some of the substance of *Genesis* about Cain's murder of his brother, Abel, though, as is said, any resemblance is purely accidental. Roughly, an initially rebellious Cain is confronted by Lucifer, taken off on a cosmic time-flight seeing past and future, and comes back again to murder his brother in a fit of rage. What makes the poem interesting is the way Byron treats all of this. He has many questions, though in the end he has no settled answers or belief; much of the poem is therefore effective as a set of ironically placed statements, leaving the reader (and Byron) in some doubt as to what to think or believe.

Cain's problem is the problem largely of inherited evil; he does not see why he should have to suffer for something that his father and mother did, nor why he should worship someone unjust enough to punish in this way. The whole system seems to him to be inescapably evil. Cain involuntarily echoes the 'serpent's words', as Eve tells him, but this does not make it follow that the snake was lying when it would be good to pluck and eat the fruit, at least not for Cain:

> The snake spoke *truth*; it *was* the tree of knowledge;
> It *was* the tree of life; knowledge is good,
> And life is good; and how can both be evil?

> I, *i*, 36–8

But all that Cain can see is that there is an ethical problem involved which seems to demonstrate a bad God; must it be that

> Because
> He is all-powerful, must all-good, too, follow?
> I judge but by the fruits—and they are bitter—
> Which I must feed on for a fault not mine.

I, i, 76–9

These thoughts of Cain are echoed to his face by Lucifer who then enters, a Lucifer who owes *something* to Milton's Satan, though he *seems* to have Cain's interests at heart. Lucifer assures Cain that he is

> One who aspired to be what made thee, and
> Would not have made thee what thou art.

I, i, 126–7

and that he and Cain are two of a kind, a confederacy against God, those

> who dare look the Omnipotent tyrant in
> His everlasting face, and tell him that
> His evil is not good!

I, i, 138–40

Over against God's 'immense existence' which he sees as 'burdensome' to Him with His 'unparticipated solitude', Lucifer erects another alternative, men and Spirits who 'sympathise'

> And, suffering in concert, make our pangs
> Innumerable more endurable,
> By the unbounded sympathy of all
> With all!

I, i, 158–61

Cain is now, for the first time, hearing his own deepest thoughts expressed by someone else, and, moreover, 'never till/Now met I aught to sympathise with me' (I, i, 186–7). As a firm clinch to the growing relationship of Lucifer's spoken words to Cain's unspoken thoughts, Lucifer echoes Cain's thinking about God's malevolence in deliberately putting temptation in his parents' way by planting the tree near Adam and Eve; Lucifer says:

116

> I tempt none,
> Save with the truth: was not the tree the tree
> Of knowledge? and was not the tree of life
> Still fruitful? Did *I* bid her pluck them not?
> Did *I* plant things prohibited within
> The reach of beings innocent, and curious
> By their own innocence?
>
> I, i, 193–9

As a positive quality, if rebellion is not positive enough, Lucifer offers a Byronic Prometheanism to Cain:

> Nothing can
> Quench the mind, if the mind will be itself
> And centre of surrounding things—'tis made
> To sway.
>
> I, ii, 210–3

But Lucifer seems a hard one; he has a harsh sarcasm which he uses from time to time, as in his sneer at religion (or religiosity):

> Higher things than ye are slaves: and higher
> Than them or ye would be so, did they not
> Prefer an independency of torture
> To the smooth agonies of adulation,
> In hymns and harpings, and self-seeking prayers,
> To that which is omnipotent, because
> It is omnipotent, and not from love,
> But terror and self-hope.
>
> I, i, 380–7

Lucifer extends the impossible choice between love and knowledge, and Cain is urged to accept love by his wife (and sister) Adah rather than knowledge. It is an impossible choice; he loves Adah and yet the children that are born of their love will be part of the innumerable generations who will inherit 'agonies accumulated'. He both knows and he loves; yet his knowledge is incomplete. At least if his parents had eaten of the tree of knowledge they ought to have all knowledge, yet no one knows Death or what it is. All they know is that they are miserable. Adah is on the side of the *status quo* and her woman's happiness is husband and family, and she is gentle, unquestioning and alive to beauty. She has a moving little speech in praise of Lucifer's beauty in terms of the night sky, gentle and indicative of her personality:

> but thou seem'st
> Like an ethereal night, where long white clouds
> Streak the deep purple, and unnumber'd stars
> Spangle the wonderful mysterious vault
> With things that look as if they would be suns;
> So beautiful, unnumber'd, and endearing,
> Not dazzling, and yet drawing us to them,
> They fill my eyes with tears, and so dost thou.
> Thou seem'st unhappy: do not make us so,
> And I will weep for thee.
>
> I, *i*, 506–15

But men must work and women must weep, so Cain goes off on his space–time flight with Lucifer playing the savage eye-opener on things and events. The journey only presents ironies and no certainty of the relationship of God and Lucifer; both an orthodox view and a more Manichean notion of 'The *two Principles*' (italicised by Byron to make sure we take the point of the idea that there are two equal and opponent powers which rule the universe, which was the Manichean heresy).

Now, after all that he has seen, Cain feels that he has only learnt that he seems Nothing, and Lucifer is coldly cynical about it all:

> And this should be the human sum
> Of knowledge, to know mortal nature's nothingness;
> Bequeath that science to thy children, and
> 'Twill spare them many tortures.
>
> II, *ii*, 421–4

The Act and the space trip end where we started with the problem of the relationship of good to evil. Lucifer seems oddly contradictory in what he says about this. The problem, simply, is:—if Good is what God calls Good, then it may be really Bad. So, Lucifer says about God:

He as a conqueror will call the conquer'd
Evil; but what will be the *good* he gives?
Were I the victor, *his* works would be deem'd
The only evil ones.

II, ii, 443–6

But he maintains an absolute standard for Good and Bad:

Evil and good are things in their own essence,
And not made good or evil by the giver;
But if he gives you good—so call him; if
Evil springs from *him*, do not name it *mine*,
Till ye know better its true fount; and judge
Not by words, though of spirits, but the fruits
Of your existence, such as it must be.

II, i, 452–8

And so we are back, with Cain, not only to the original statement of the problem but to Cain's very words before Lucifer
appeared on the scene at all.

And in this new appreciation of ironies Cain is, in the last Act,
back with his family 'near Eden'. Cain sees his baby son who
will have to 'be amerced for sins unknown' dreaming of Paradise, though a 'disinherited boy'. Psychologically he is ready for
any spark to send him up in a blaze, and Abel is at hand to do
just that. When Adah tells him that Abel has left two altars ready
for sacrifice Cain explodes. He shouts his anger at God; he
shouts at Abel's presumption that Cain will be as servile as
himself; he screams at the notion of having to sacrifice on top of
having the curse of God to endure, as if that was not enough;
and, finally, he is incensed at the idea of the suffering to come on
the innocent, both themselves and Enoch and his children.

And then Abel comes along to offer sacrifice. Cain tries not
to offend his brother by attempting to avoid both the sacrifice
itself and his own anger at his brother. He cannot escape, but
has to listen to Abel's prayer, complementary to his stance of
abasement before God. Abel accepts his sin (though Cain would
count him 'innocent') and so can say, for example:

119

And spared, despite our father's sin, to make
His children all lost, as they might have been,
Had not thy justice been so temper'd with
The mercy which is thy delight, as to
Accord a pardon like a Paradise,
Compared with our great crimes.

III, i, 226-31

No doubt antagonised by this attitude of servility Cain stands and himself antagonises God; his altar has no blood or spilt life (the irony of a merciful God being pleased with slaughter no doubt in Cain's mind):

If a shrine without victim,
And altar without gore, may win thy favour,
Look on it! and for him who dresseth it,
He is—such as thou mad'st him; and seeks nothing
Which must be won by kneeling:

III, i, 266-70

He returns to his old theme and problem of God's will and the Good:

and good and evil seem
To have no power themselves, save in thy will;
And whether that be good or ill I know not,
Not being omnipotent, nor fit to judge
Omnipotence, but merely to endure
Its mandate;

III, i, 274-9

Now there is action. Cain's sacrifice is scattered by a wind; he is angered at God who accepts blood and not fruits and he wants to overturn Abel's altar. Abel, of course, refuses, and Cain takes a brand from the fire and wounds him fatally. There are long distracted speeches about Death, highly anachronistic in their use of terms like 'fatally', 'murder', 'fratricide', and Cain at last comes to his senses when he is alone:

I am awake at last—a dreary dream
Had madden'd me;—

III, i, 378-9

Eve curses Cain with a terrible curse and he is turned away by all except his wife, Adah, including the Angel of the Lord.

What is striking about the poem after the murder has been committed is Cain's awakening to the fact of his having killed his brother whom he loved and who loved him, and he takes on something of the gentle quality that the Angel attributed to Abel:

> Stern thou hast been and stubborn from the womb,
> As the ground thou must henceforth till; but he
> Thou slew'st was gentle as the flocks he tended.
>
> III, i, 503-5

And so, Cain's last speech is neither of self-pity nor of defiance or anger at God's judgment, but of pity for the dead Abel:

> I
> Have dried the fountain of a gentle race,
> Which might have graced his recent marriage couch,
> And might have temper'd this stern blood of mine,
> Uniting with our children Abel's offspring!
>
> III, i, 557-60

This leaves us with the problem of what we are to make of the real nature of Cain, the relationship of Cain the murderer to Cain the rebel. Are we to say that it was because he was deluded by Lucifer, speaking aloud Cain's inner thoughts, and encouraging rebellion against God, that Cain eventually killed his brother? Are we to say that Cain's intellectual revolt stands, even though he now may be a fratricide? Byron does not say; and one might conclude that Byron does not carry out a propagandist programme to the end. Cain, in rebelling against God, destroys his brother, rather than rescuing him from his servility to the Omnipotent tyrant.

What one can say is that Byron's own attitudes come out plainly enough: his hatred of servility (his Satanic *non serviam*); his own feeling of hauteur and separateness from the believing mob; his dislike of slaughter and needless cruelty; his sympathy with bereavement and his love of gentleness in women.

One could say that intellectually this poem was a bit of a

muddle, but this would be wrong. Byron knows the problems; he knows some of the puzzling questions, but he has no theological certainty. He neither believes nor disbelieves; he uses irony to get round his having to come down on one side or the other. Sometimes one is in sympathy with Cain, and sometimes intellectually with Lucifer. The reader and Cain are both misled and yet told 'the truth'.

'HEAVEN AND EARTH: A MYSTERY'

In the same year as *Cain*, 1821, Byron wrote *Heaven and Earth*, again from *Genesis*, but this time his imagination was caught by the notion of love between the 'sons of God' and the 'daughters of men'. The poem has an epigraph from Coleridge's *Kubla Khan*, 'By woman wailing for her demon lover'. This was an interesting insight on the Byronic theme of forbidden love, and the women he involves are of the descendants of Cain, and so destined for destruction in the coming Flood, while the chief protagonist is Japhet who is destined to be saved, willy-nilly.

What we have is, supposedly, the first part of an unfinished poem, though one is hard put to know where we would go next after the Flood. The story as we have it is confused enough, and there is no clear theological line at all. The women and their lovers, though they form an essential part of the poem, really exist so that Japhet can respond to their imminent destruction (they escape with their Angelic lovers, absent without leave from the Heavenly Court, and their ultimate fate is left in doubt). In Scene iii Japhet has a long soliloquy showing his distress at the prospect of the obliteration of a known and loved world by the coming Flood, reaching a peak of rhetorical flourish and anger at his thinking of Noah's preservation of 'creeping things' at God's word:

> May
> *He* preserve *them*, and I *not* have the power
> To snatch the loveliest of earth's daughters from
> A doom which even some serpent, with his mate,
> Shall 'scape to save his kind to be prolong'd,
> To hiss and sting through some emerging world,

Reeking and dank from out the slime, whose ooze
Shall slumber o'er the wreck of this, until
The salt morass subside into a sphere,
Beneath the sun, and be the monument,
The sole and undistinguish'd sepulchre,
Of yet quick myriads of all life?

iii, 36–46

Evil spirits come to mock and laugh at Japhet for his baseness in seeking to escape destruction, and, after having said that they will be glad to see the end of man, no more prayers, no more adoration to annoy them, they echo Japhet's own words. The few undestroyed beings are to be a

remnant, floating o'er the undulation
Of the subsiding deluge, from its slime,
When the hot sun hath baked the reeking soil
Into a world, shall give again to Time
New beings—years, diseases, sorrow, crime . . .

iii, 187–91

Japhet tries to offer the consolation of a future redemption, but the spirits reply with a sort of *Childe Harold's Pilgrimage's* (Canto IV style) version of life; nothing changes:

The same old tears, old crimes, and oldest ill
Shall be amongst your race in different forms;
    But the same moral storms
Shall oversweep the future, as the waves
In a few hours the glorious giants' graves.

iii, 213–17

Again, the spirits re-enact the Lucifer/Cain situation by accusing God (implicitly) of shocking cruelty—killing beautiful creatures. Cain's sons will all die:

And all his goodly daughters
    Must lie beneath the desolating waters;
Or, floating upward, with their long hair laid
Along the wave, the cruel heaven upbraid.

iii, 256–9

Japhet then meets the women with their Angelic lovers who seem not to know the doom, and tries to persuade the Angels to save the women. Aholibamah, the true Cainite, is as haughty as ever her ancestor was, and is proud in

> that haughty blood which springs
> From him who shed the first, and that a brother's!

iii, 398–9

Anah, the one whom Japhet loves unrequited, echoes the demonic wish not to live exempted from the doom, not that she does not fear for her life, but (talking to her sister)

> What were the world, or other worlds, or all
> The brightest future, without the sweet past—
> Thy love, my father's, all the life, and all
> The things which sprang up with me, like the stars,
> Making my dim existence radiant with
> Soft lights which were not mine?

iii, 434–9

Such a moving statement cannot come, one is made to feel, from someone so evil as to deserve obliteration; there are all the obviously good qualities of love, admiration, delight in nature's beauty, and these are brought to bear on the earlier demonic argument.

Noah and Shem enter, rather like policemen, and upbraid Japhet. Raphael comes and announces that the Seraphs must either return to duty or forfeit eternal bliss. Nothing, he says, can be saved, though he is not above demonstrating his admiration for the former beauty of Satan and his regret that the fall of the angels ever happened. So the Seraphs stand by their lovers and take them off when the deluge comes.

As the water rises we have a Chorus of Mortals with varied responses to the situation; in fact, there are many shades of theology involved. There is the simple prayer to God to be saved, the mother's cursing God because she cannot see why her unweaned baby should die, the refusal to bend the knee to God as we are going to die anyway and nothing can change that, the mocking of Japhet who will be saved and then he will be able to see 'The corpses of the world of thy young days' and then he can praise Jehovah, and, finally, the man of faith who refuses 'for a little gasp of breath' to 'blaspheme and groan'.

The poem ends with Japhet's recognition that for him survival is worse than extinction; he will have to

> behold the universal tomb
> Which I
> Am thus condemn'd to weep above in vain.
> Why, when all perish, why must I remain?

iii, 926–9

The only thing clear about the poem's theology, compared with *Cain*, is the notion of God's arbitrary predestination of individuals. Japhet is told by Raphael that he is to be saved as Noah's son, and that is all. The variety of response makes the theology a 'mystery' for the rest of the poem. As a human story it has its moments, though few.

9

'Italy's a Pleasant Place': Italian Poems

'THE LAMENT OF TASSO'

Among Byron's responses to Italy were poems which he wrote which could never have been written without Italy as a context. We have seen one of his major responses to Italy as a land of poetry and former freedom in *Childe Harold IV*, but there were other poetic responses and among the first of them was *The Lament of Tasso*. It was written before *Childe Harold IV*, though in the same year.

It presents an extreme case of the lone poet in the extremity of rejection by men and with an impossible but sustaining love. This brings in mind the later *Childe Harold's Pilgrimage*, though the love in this case is a purely imaginary one, and it is through his imagination that the poet survives his solitary confinement in a madhouse. In one sense the poet needed an unfulfillable love:

> from my very birth
> My soul was drunk with love, which did pervade
> And mingle with whate'er I saw on earth:

149–51

and then, as a man, his whole heart was

> exalted into One Want,
> But undefined and wandering, till the day
> I found the thing I sought—and that was thee: . . .

168–70

The fact that his love for Leonora was unrequited and made impossible the fulfilment is now his salvation, his one means of sanity.

126

The poet loved solitude and so, in a sense again, he is in his *ideal* situation; but now his mind is going, and perhaps this is his punishment for loving as he does:

> Why in this furnace is my spirit proved,
> Like steel in tempering fire? because I loved?
> Because I loved what not to love, and see,
> Was more or less than mortal, and than me.

204-7

But all this is conditional on his poet's imagination, and he has sustained himself so long in solitary confinement just because his is a poet's love, an ideal and not a reality, past or present, with nothing in it to warrant there having been a history of meetings, mutual sighs, endearments, and so on:

> That thou wert beautiful, and I not blind,
> Hath been the sin which shuts me from mankind;
> But let them go, or torture as they will,
> My heart can multiply thy image still . . .

55-8

Now the ageing poet is fighting against madness and he will not commit suicide because his name would suffer; his concern as a poet is with the future, a future which his prophetic vision sees where his renown will be high and the state of Ferrara, his unjust city, as low as its 'unpeopled walls', and his cell as a consecrated spot. His ideal love, Leonora, will then have

> One half the laurel which o'ershades my grave.

This little poem is one where Byron is able to sympathise with the long-dead and majestic poet by seeing him as embodying some of the notions of art which Byron himself was then thinking about, a curiously Romantic figure, but having a fierce attachment to art and the imagination as more than pleasant pastimes. There is a passion and energy in the poem which derives, one supposes, from the basic relationships that one, or Byron, might draw from the nature of the two rejected wandering poets separated from their ideal loves.

That other wandering poetic outlaw, Shelley, certainly

responded to the situation, and in a letter to Byron he wrote:

> There are passages, indeed, most wonderfully impressive; and those lines in which you describe the youthful feelings of Tasso; that indistinct consciousness of its own greatness, which a heart of genius cherishes in solitude, amid neglect and contempt, have a profound and thrilling pathos which I will confess to you, whenever I turn to them, make my head wild with tears.
>
> LORD BYRON'S CORRESPONDENCE II, 59

'THE PROPHECY OF DANTE'

Whereas the Tasso poem was written in an English measure, basically the couplet, though free and flowing, showing that common breakdown of the strict form which one might also see, for example, in Keats's *Endymion* (1818), the next Italian poem, *The Prophecy of Dante*, is in Italian *terza rima*, Dante's measure.

Of course, Byron is careful to point this out in his preface, and to suggest that it be treated as a 'metrical experiment'. Well, this it is, and one can say that the verse is usually competent, at times good and fluent, but at times tortured to make English fit the Italian form. The form is a linking of the rhyme in a continuous flow (ababcbcdc), but we must not let this Dantean form fool us into thinking that Byron is really talking like Dante. For, just as Tasso becomes a Romantic poet, so this poem becomes a poem about poets and poetry and about Liberty, political liberty.

The poem opens, rather like our first poem, with an old man celebrating his ideal love for the famous Beatrice:

> love so ineffable, and so alone,
> That nought on earth could more my bosom move.
>
> I, 21-2

His mind is indomitable; he is alienated from men and from his native city, though he has a great love for that city which cursed him:

128

Alas! how bitter is his country's curse
To him who *for* that country would expire,
 But did not merit to expire *by* her,
 And loves her, loves her even in her ire!

I, 69–72

He is too old and too full of bitter human experience for anything to remain but Despair, feeling that he is 'not of this people,
nor this age', and, like all Byronic protagonists,

       'tis the doom
 Of spirits of my order to be rack'd
In life, to wear their hearts out, and consume
 Their days in endless strife, and die alone . . .

I, 149–52

Still, he is free, and, almost inevitably, an exile.

The second canto is a lament for Italy, subjugated by the
Goths in the past, and now the future will see 'the German,
Frank, and Hun'. We now feel that we have moved right into
Byron's own time in Italy, for the question is: Why must this
be? What could be done? The answer is given in terms which
should have been the rallying-cry in the divided Italy Byron
saw:

 What is there wanting then to set thee free,
  And show thy beauty in its fullest light?
  To make the Alps impassable; and we,
 Her sons, may do this with *one* deed—
  Unite.

II, 142–5

Canto III looks at the poets who are to come after Dante,
and there is a direct link made between poetry and the inspiration
to political freedom, though, the prophecy runs, only a few will
escape being tied to 'some small prince/In all the prodigality of
praise!' (III, 74–5). Petrarch is lauded, as are Ariosto and Tasso
who 'will both consume/In penury and pain too many a year'
(150–1), and who will die in despondency and yet bequeath

To the kind world, which scarce will yield a tear,
A heritage enriching all who breathe
    With the wealth of a genuine poet's soul . . .

III, 153–5

The specifically Italian nature is dropped, finally, for a lament for all poets, for their inevitable destruction, a typically Romantic regret (and expressing a typical Romantic notion of poetry):

Must all the finer thoughts, the thrilling sense,
    The electric blood with which their arteries run,
Their body's self turned soul with the intense
    Feeling of that which is, and fancy of
    That which should be, to such a recompense
Conduct?

III, 161–6

In the following canto there is a much plainer Romantic statement about poets and the nature of poetry: it is a matter of the intense feeling and a special function which defines a poet, not his quality of verse:

Many are poets but without the name,
    For what is poesy but to create,
    From overfeeling good or ill; and aim
At an external life beyond our fate,
    And be the new Prometheus of new men,
    Bestowing fire from heaven, and then, too late,
Finding the pleasure given repaid with pain,
    And vultures to the heart of the bestower, . . .

IV, 10–17

This sort of apologia brings into mind immediately Wordsworth's celebrated sentence from his *Preface to Lyrical Ballads* (1802), paragraph 6;

For all good poetry is the spontaneous overflow of powerful feelings: and though this were true, Poems to which any value can be attached were never produced on any variety of subjects but by a man who, being possessed of more than usual organic sensibility, had also thought long and deeply.

Just as importantly, we must think of Shelley's notion of the poet as the 'legislator of the world' and his definition of the poet's Promethean role in his *Defence of Poetry*. But it is not all Wordsworth and Shelley; there is Byron's own recognition of the inability of man to recognise and accept the poet's 'fire from heaven'.

After praise of the artistic productions in Italy in coming time, an 'Age of Beauty', in spite of destruction by tyrants, the poem returns to thoughts about poets, great poets, the 'sons of fame', and their lot who

> Must pass their days in penury or pain,
> Or step to grandeur through the paths of shame,
> And wear a deeper brand and gaudier chain . . .
>
> IV, 104–6

Or, if they are 'born aloof/From lowliness' (like Byron, one thinks) then they have to sustain 'The inner war of passions deep and fierce' (110). The shade of all those passion-torn heroes flits over the poem, and then it ends with a final calm with the old irreconcilable poet separated for ever from his native Florence, and who will die alone

> Beholding with the dark eye of a seer
> The evil days to gifted souls foreshown,
> Foretelling them to those who will not hear.
>
> IV, 149–51

This seems a rather weak end, and perhaps the trouble is that the poem is neither simply a set of predictions, prophet-like or Cassandra-like, but thoughts about poetry, its nature, its relation to politics, and thoughts about Italian shortsightedness.

It does seem worth while to point up the notion, expressed here, that poetry seems not to be something written down, but a poet can be any major artist of whatever medium; a doctrine which flourished in Romantic mouths and still remains with us today.

About this poem Shelley was more cautious, but giving us the impression that he understood the talk about the political and prophetic nature of poetry, being a natural prophet himself, a hater of systems and tyranny:

> The poetry of this piece is indeed sublime; and if it have not general admiration, you ought still to be contented; because the subject, no less than the style, is addressed to the few, and, like some of the highest passages in 'Childe Harold', will only be *fully* appreciated by the select readers of many generations.
>
> LORD BYRON'S CORRESPONDENCE II, 200

And here we are.

'ODE ON VENICE'

This poem, written in 1818, the year of the publication of Canto IV of *Childe Harold's Pilgrimage*, repeats something of the sentiments expressed there about Venice and about freedom. Venice is seen as the past mother of freedom, and, now, all free Europe has either submitted to tyranny or is likely to submit, even Holland, and perhaps Switzerland because

> tyranny of late is cunning grown,
> And in its own good season tramples down
> The sparkles of our ashes.
>
> 131–3

The hope of the free world is now America (*plus ça change*); she has taught that England's flag

> May strike to those whose red right hands have bought
> Rights cheaply earn'd with blood.
>
> 147–8

Freedom needs 'red right hands' and

> the few spirits, who, despite of deeds
> Which they abhor, confound not with the cause
> Those momentary starts from Nature's laws,
> Which, like the pestilence and earthquake, smite
> But for a term . . .
>
> 92–6

And Byron is seeing revolution in terms which are not simply idealistic, steeling himself to recognise the things that must be accomplished to regain freedom from tyranny.

The conclusion of the poem is a splendid piece of Byronic rhetorical writing, and goes some way to showing how thrilling this sort of writing could be in an explosive situation, as it was then in Italy, ripe for rebellion:

> Still, still, for ever,
> Better, though each man's life-blood were a river,
> That it should flow, and overflow, than creep
> Through thousand lazy channels in our veins,
> Damm'd like the dull canal with locks and chains,
> And moving, as a sick man in his sleep,
> Three paces, and then faltering: better be
> Where the extinguish'd Spartans still are free,
> In their proud charnel of Thermopylae,
> Than stagnate in our marsh,—or o'er the deep
> Fly, and one current to the ocean add,
> One spirit to the souls our fathers had,
> One freeman more, America, to thee!

148–60

'FRANCESCA OF RIMINI'

A feature of Byron's life in Italy was his increasing interest in its literature, and he did for some time seriously contemplate writing in Italian as his literary medium. Out of this interest come several translations from the Italian, and *Francesca of Rimini* is a translation from Dante's *Inferno*, one of the most famous episodes in Dante's work.

What is interesting about the translation is that Byron was trying his hand at a line for line and rhyme for rhyme translation, and called it 'cramp English' when writing to his publisher, Murray, about it in March 1820.

The episode, though naturally awkward in parts, does show a situation which is appealing to Byron, and one which engages his sympathies as well as Dante's; and one can quite see, in the context of Byron's poetry dealing with love, that sympathy is involved in

Alas! unto such ill
How many sweet thoughts, what strong ecstasies,
Led these their evil fortune to fulfill!

16–18

'BEPPO'

It is a bit indecent to take this poem as one of a group of Italian poems, but as it was modelled on the style of the serio-comic Italian poet, Pulci, it may as well come in here.

It is curious, but true, that one of the major turning points in Byron's career is marked by his reading of a poem by John Hookham Frere, *The Monks and the Giants,* under the pseudonym of Whistlecraft. In this poem Frere had adapted the *Morgante Maggiore* of Luigi Pulci, a 15th-century Florentine poet who had reduced the chivalric tale to a farce by his racy Florentine dialectal idioms and a style dazzling with its ludicrousness and involvement of rhyme and expression. His vehicle had been the *ottava rima,* an extremely flexible stanza form with alternate rhymes ending in a couplet (abababcc). Pulci found the possibilities of humorous use of the couplet and of the whole deflationary range the stanza had.

'Whistlecraft' discovered this for an English audience, among whom was Byron. He was at the time writing supplementary stanzas for Canto IV of *Childe Harold's Pilgrimage,* and he saw before him the verse form that would allow him to express himself, no longer as Pilgrim or Brigand or Broken Heart, but as the Byron of the letters his friends knew. Here was a form of verse where he could support his variety of responses to the world, amused, slamming, laudatory, comic or serious, bawdy or disdainful. What he had lost from his poetry we can see from his letters contemporaneous with that more solemn and 'artificial' way of writing, his courtdress, letters which are at once energetic and unbuttoned. Now he could be himself and not a *persona* adopted (and expected) by the public.

Beppo was composed during September and early October 1817, and on October 12 he wrote to Murray:

I have written a poem (of 84 octave stanzas) humorous, in or after the excellent manner of Mr. Whistlecraft (whom I take to be Frere), on a Venetian anecdote which amused me.

The story itself, the basic anecdote, would take only a few sentences to tell, and would seem a trivial story in the best of mouths. A man, presumed dead because he had been away at sea for so long, returns home to find his wife and her lover at a ball. He goes to his house and confronts them; they go in and take coffee and conclude with a *ménage à trois*. And that's all.

Byron's interest in the story is the simple Italian quality it displays (and the fact that, as it was told him, it was vouched for as true) and the opportunity it gives him to display Italian attitudes and sentiments, particularly the ideas of sexuality. This gives him a parallel opportunity to see English attitudes in comparison, colder and more hypocritical, and to explore *mores* in general, amusing to the bystander, the universal traveller. In doing all this he can be as relaxed and talkative as he pleases, talking for talking's sake, with no thought of reiterating a theme or a moral, just Lord Byron talking with fascination in his mobility of mood.

Frere's poem was colloquial to a greater extent than his Italian models, and his rhymes are sometimes daring (oddities/body 'tis; surpass us/Parnassus; the giants/King Ryence); he had included reference to contemporary people and interests (which the Italian did not) and he had relaxed the stanzaic form. Byron took all this much further and made his own instrument for his own voice, a voice which *speaks* and does not posture or take up a special rhetorical stance with one hand on the heart or forehead and the other directed at the unseen audience.

The poem opens miles away from the story with the Carnival, a celebration deliciously ludicrous to a spectator (English); people let themselves go, 'And buy repentance, ere they grow devout'

> With fiddling, feasting, dancing, drinking, masking,
> And other things which may be had for asking.

i

Innuendo and exhilaration lie cheek by jowl, and we get used to such conflicts and switches throughout this splendidly lively poem. During the celebrations everyone dresses up, but Heaven help you if you use clerical dress; the ecclesiastics will haul

> you o'er the coals, and stir the fires
> Of Phlegethon with every mother's son,

and you could not get them to

> say one mass to cool the cauldron's bubble
> That boil'd your bones, unless you paid them double.

iv

Here colloquialism, learned reference and side-swipe at venality occur with the first ever jocular use of an echo from *Macbeth*, surely a real demonstration of how far Byron is moving away from all his poetry so far written. We can note the same thing again in Stanza lxvi, much later in the poem, where the lady is tearing other ladies to pieces at the ball:

> And lo! an eighth appears,—'I'll see no more!'
> For fear, like Banquo's kings, they reach a score.

Byron loves Italy and knows his Italians but if you are thinking of coming to Italy just now you will find Lent on, and that means no meat, just fish without sauce, so he recommends that you ride or walk to the Strand

> and buy in gross
> (Or if set out beforehand, these may send
> By any means least liable to loss)
> Ketchup, Soy, Chili-vinegar, and Harvey,
> Or by the Lord! a Lent will well nigh starve ye . . .

viii

That magical ability to say in spoken English just what you want to and yet in verse is so pronounced in this poem that we must recognise a real master.

One thing that the poem has is Byron's finest cool responses to England in all his poetic output; he can be witty, urbane, varying his tone from confidential to musing, from mockery to irony, from his characterisation of 'budding misses' to his long catalogue of 'these I have loved' (*xlvii–xlix*), (which one ought, perhaps, to set beside Rupert Brooke's poem more fully to appreciate Byron's coolness and quietly destructive satire). His English rosebuds are remembered acutely and, perhaps, accurately:

> 'Tis true, your budding Miss is very charming,
>> But shy and awkward at first coming out,
> So much alarm'd, that she is quite alarming,
>> All Giggle, Blush; half Pertness, and half Pout;
> And glancing at *Mamma*, for fear there's harm in
>> What you, she, it, or they, may be about,
> The nursery still lisps out in all they utter—
> Besides, they always smell of bread and butter.
>
> xxxix

The poem is really all, officially, 'digression', and Byron cannot help it, once he is talking then he is talking. He mocks the reader when he brings himself back to his tale, 'But to my tale of Laura—', and then off he is again, warning himself that as he finds digression becoming tedious then so will his reader; then, turning half-aside with a mock-seriousness, can say:

> The gentle reader, who may wax unkind,
>> And caring little for the author's ease,
> Insist on knowing what he means, a hard
> And hapless situation for a bard.
>
> l

All is available for mockery, himself included. He is one of those authors who have gained fame from the 'Oriental Tale' (as we have seen); and now if only he had 'the art of easy writing' (as if this is not the easiest writing we have met), then he would scale Parnassus where the Muses

> sit inditing
> Those pretty poems never known to fail.
> How quickly would I print (the world delighting)
>> A Grecian, Syrian, or Assyrian tale,

And sell you, mix'd with western sentimentalism,
Some samples of the finest Orientalism.

li

This new and importantly different poetic Byron is *par excellence* the Byron of *Don Juan,* but he comes to life here, a little quietly facetious on everything, and certainly just as much engaged with his own image as Childe Harold or the Giaour. Here he wants to be seen with a rhyming knack and a scorn for the professional writer and critic. Gone are the others with their stature, rhetoric, doom and self-importance; now we are asked to see

> but a nameless sort of person,
>   (A broken Dandy lately on my travels)
> And take for rhyme, to hook my rambling verse on,
>   The first that Walker's Lexicon unravels,
> And when I can't find that, I put a worse on,
>   Not caring as I ought for critics' cavils;
> I've half a mind to tumble down to prose,
> But verse is more in fashion—so here goes.

lii

There are two things here that must not be forgotten: Byron did care what critics *he* respected thought and was more than willing to listen to them at times, and Byron thought a good deal about his rhymes and spent a very great deal of time and effort on this poem. On the first point we might remember that both Hobhouse and his friend Gifford, the famous critic of Byron's time, were asked to read a set of proofs of *Childe Harold's Pilgrimage IV.* Both made suggestions for alterations and excisions. In a letter to Hobhouse of 5 March 1818, Byron wrote:

> I am however, greatly obliged by G.'s suggestions, which are well meant, and generally well grounded, and surely good-natured as can be; and one ought to attend to the opinions of a man whose critical talent swept down a whole host of writers at once; I don't mean from *fear,* but from real respect for the sense of his observations.

LORD BYRON'S CORRESPONDENCE II, 69

Overleaf, the editor, John Murray, who had the manuscripts, notes:

> Gifford's notes are especially interesting. Almost without exception they suggest some striking improvement and were accepted by Byron.
>
> IBID, 70

On the second point a critic, Guy Steffan, has shown several most illuminating things from his study of Byron's extant first draft MS. He demonstrates the ways in which the original 84 stanzas grew into the 99 that we have, and some of his statistics are almost staggering. In the MS. revision there were, for example, 417 major revisions, 235 verbal or phrasal substitutions, and about 37 per cent of all manuscript stanzas have four or more lines revised. He shows the way that Byron strove for energy and activity in expression as a compensation for the lack of actual movement in the story, and certainly demonstrates beyond all shadow of doubt the pains and literary effort that Byron expended on this most easy-seeming of poems, this work of an 'Improvisatore'.

But still, for the poem's sake, we enjoy the satire of

> One hates an author that's *all author*, fellows
>   In foolscap uniforms turn'd up with ink,
> So very anxious, clever, fine, and jealous.
>   One don't know what to say to them, or think,
> Unless to puff them with a pair of bellows;
>   Of coxcombry's worst coxcombs e'en the pink
> Are preferable to these shreds of paper,
> These unquench'd snuffings of the midnight taper.
>
> *lxxv*

Bluestockings are smacked down later, including those ladies who indulge in mathematics (a private joke against his wife, the 'Princess of Parallelograms', as he called her); Moslem women are spared so many things and

> They stare not on the stars from out their attics,
> Nor deal (thank God for that!) in mathematics.
>
> *lxxviii*

And in the following stanza he catches himself at the satirist's game and sighs a mock sigh, only to characterise his real bent only too successfully, and, incidentally, show how his thought demanded a medium that can rise and fall suddenly, to be grave and gay almost in the same breath:

> I fear I have a little turn for satire,
>   And yet methinks the older that one grows
> Inclines us more to laugh than scold, though laughter
> Leaves us so doubly serious shortly after.

lxxi

But one must not think that the poem is all Byron; it is not. He gives a resounding verbal picture of Laura by her talk embedded in a context of rich irony where English women are seen by contrast with their Italian sisters. When Laura and her *cavaliere servente* learn that the strange Turk who had so taken Laura's eye at the Ridotto is none other than her husband, Beppo, Laura behaves as an Italian and not an English woman. Instead of throwing a faint she, like Italian women in general, saves

> much hartshorn, salts, and sprinkling faces
> And cutting stays, as usual in such cases.

lxxxix

So the three all go into the palace for coffee in a 'civilised' way, but Laura talks to her long-lost husband just as though he has been away on a long trip and has come home expected but a little altered by all that foreign travel:

> 'Beppo! that beard of yours becomes you not;
>   It shall be shaved before you're a day older:
> Why do you wear it? Oh! I had forgot—
>   Pray don't you think the weather here is colder?
> How do I look? You shan't stir from that spot
>   In that queer dress, for fear that some beholder
> Should find you out, and make the story known.
> How short your hair is! Lord! how grey it's grown!'

xciii

So much to enjoy here, but it might just be worth noting

how Byron's voice catches a woman's, its running on out of gear, its lunatic logic (coming out of disguise will shout the story abroad!) and how we can hear the woman getting closer and closer to the man until she's almost falling into his lap. Excellent theatre; the handling of conversation of this naturalness is something that he has not allowed himself in verse before, and we might bear in mind Byron's earlier reporting at the Ridotto. The women are watching the long file of men passing Laura and all bowing and smiling at her:

> The women only thought it quite amazing
>   That, at her time of life, so many were
> Admirers still,—but men are so debased,
> Those brazen creatures always suit their taste.
>
> lxvii

And so we have the first step in Byron's development of the final poetic manner, that manner perfected in *Don Juan*, a drawing into poetry of that part of Byron which one can see in his letters and in his *jeux d'esprit* which enlivened his prose letters occasionally. Now he was poetically mature as a poet and had found a medium which suited that maturity and his inability to maintain one attitude for long, an experiment and prelude to the greater *Don Juan*, but it stands in its own right and is one of the liveliest and unboring poems in our language, a tribute to Byron's love for and happiness in Italy,

> With all its sinful doings, I must say,
>   That Italy's a pleasant place to me . . .
>
> xli

THE 'MORGANTE MAGGIORE'

One of the side effects of Byron's stimulation by Frere was a reading of Pulci in Italian, and this issued in a translation of the first canto of Pulci's poem, *Morgante Maggiore*. When Byron wrote to Hobhouse about it he said that he had sent Murray

> a translation, close and rugged, of the first canto of the Morgante Maggiore, to be published with the original text, side by side, 'cheek by jowl gome,' on account of the superlative merits of both.
> LORD BYRON'S CORRESPONDENCE II, 136

In his preface to the translation Byron says that he was induced into the experiment

> partly by his love for, and partial intercourse with, the Italian language, of which it is so easy to acquire a slight knowledge, and with which it is so nearly impossible for a foreigner to become accurately conversant.

His having achieved this degree of competence was a source of great pride with him and he remained far too attached to this translation during the rest of his life. It cannot be compared to *Beppo* for liveliness or for skill, and the rhyming is never so cleverly outrageous or really deflationary. As an example we might quote Stanza xxxviii to see the comparison:

> And hurl'd a fragment of size so large,
> > That if it had in fact fulfill'd its mission,
> And Roland not avail'd him of his targe,
> > There would have been no need of a physician.
> Orlando set himself in turn to charge,
> > And in his bulky bosom made incision
> With all his sword. The lout fell; but o'er thrown, he
> However by no means forgot Macone.

One of the few things that one could notice from the poem is what Byron found of the possibilities of satire and the ludicrous; the comment on the monks is suggestive for Byron's method:

> The monks, who saw the water fresh and good,
> > Rejoiced, but much more to perceive the pork;
> All animals rejoice at sight of food;
> > They lay their breviaries to sleep, and work
> With greedy pleasure, and in such a mood,
> > That the flesh needs no salt beneath their fork.
> Of rankness and of rot there is no fear,
> For all the fasts are now left in arrear.   *lxvi*

But, on the whole, the translation is only interesting because it shows how much Byron himself brought to Pulci's stanza and style, and the relation between Byron and 'the sire of the half-serious rhyme'.

142

10

'The Vision of Judgment'

In 1821, the year of the plays *Sardanapalus* and *The Two Foscari*, and the mysteries *Cain* and *Heaven and Earth*, Byron wrote a parody counterblast to what he considered a sycophantic poem on the death of the late King George III, Southey's *A Vision of Judgment*. It was written, Byron said, to Hobhouse as 'by way of reversing rogue Southey's, in my finest, ferocious, Caravaggio style . . .' (Letter to Hobhouse of 12 October 1821, *Lord Byron's Correspondence* II, 203). (What Byron might have had in mind is something of the sort of thing said by Berenson about Caravaggio's panache:

> Almost any canvas was attributed to him that was startlingly lit, that represented figures with plumed hats, vulgar obese giants blasphemously posing as Christ and His disciples, dice-throwing or card-sharping undermen, jumbles of over-jolly, swilling, embracing males and females, or more decorous musical parties.
>
> Bernard Berenson, CARAVAGGIO: HIS INCONGRUITY AND HIS FAME, Introduction)

The poem was sent to Murray on 4 October and set in type and proofs were corrected, but Murray hesitated and delayed over publication, and, a year later, Byron gave the poem to John Hunt for publication in the first number of his paper, *The Liberal*. The poem was published and Hunt duly tried and found guilty of calumniating the late King on 19 July 1824.

But Byron's intention was not simply to parody a poem he found ridiculous; he had a definite political motive in uttering a satire such as this. When all the fuss was raging about the poem he wrote to Kinnaird on 2 May 1822:

> As to myself, I shall not be deterred by an outcry. They hate me, and I detest them, I mean your present public, but they shall not interrupt the march of my mind, nor prevent me from telling the tyrants who are attempting to trample upon all thought, that their thrones will yet be rocked to their foundation.
>
> LORD BYRON'S CORRESPONDENCE II, 223

This sort of evidence must persuade us into looking for something of substance in the poem, some deep anger and political concern.

In the Preface, which did not appear when the poem was first published in *The Liberal*, Byron attacks Southey, as Southey had, in fact, attacked Byron by implication in his Preface as the leader of the 'Satanic School'. Byron says the

> gross flattery, the dull impudence, the renegado intolerance, and impious cant, of the poem by the author of 'Wat Tyler', are something so stupendous as to form the sublime of himself—containing the quintessence of his own attributes.

Southey is seen as the arch-renegade who, having written in support of a regicide and thus of liberty and popular freedom, now lavishly extols a regime and a monarch which are, for Byron, tyrannous, having caused bloodshed in America, Ireland and France. Southey is seen as an informer in his attack on the 'Satanic School', for that is where he once was himself, and Southey's attack returns on his own head.

The poem itself consists of 106 stanzas of *ottava rima* and turns on the case for admitting King George into heaven, conducted outside the gates of heaven between Satan and the Archangel Michael.

The poem opens with St. Peter nearly out of work;

> His keys were rusty, and the lock was dull,
> So little trouble had been given of late;

i

and

> The angels all were singing out of tune,
> And hoarse with having little else to do.

ii

But this levity of tone and the lightness of touch belie the gravity of the human situation where the earth is filled with a 'rapidity of vice and woe', and the recording angel, together with his newly-drafted helpers in the emergency situation, six angels and twelve saints, could hardly keep up with their work:

> So many conquerors' cars were daily driven,
>   So many kingdoms fitted up anew;
>
> *v*

'Fitted up' is so neutral a word, suggesting the fitting up of an apartment, redecoration and so on, that callousness is well conveyed. But, after getting used to the daily slaughter of six or seven thousand, the rapid scribblers threw down their pens in 'divine disgust' at 'the crowning carnage, Waterloo'.

All this is both historical background and a backcloth against which the reign of this dead sovereign must be seen in the poem, and so, after a 'hollow peace' George III dies, more madman than tyrant, more gentleman farmer than king. And yet Byron manages to convey a complex response to this king:

> A better farmer ne'er brush'd dew from lawn,
>   A worse king never left a realm undone!
>
> *viii*

An odd sort of farmer, one supposes, and the king is made to seem a pathetic figure who nevertheless was a cause of the corruption of his country, though the implication is that his ministers are the real villains. This becomes quite plain in the following stanzas on the funeral where the corpse is only an excuse for a State Funeral, where there is 'no great dearth/Of aught but tears', and where all is paid for by the State, official expenses of a 'sepulchral melodrame'.

> Who cared about the corpse? The funeral
>   Made the attraction, and the black the woe.
> There throbb'd not there a thought which pierced the pall;
>   And when the gorgeous coffin was laid low,
> It seem'd the mockery of hell to fold
> The rottenness of eighty years in gold.
>
> *x*

This again brings out Byron's complex attitude, his indication of the almost savage irony in the funeral, his disgust both at the 'rottenness' in the 'gorgeous coffin' and at the complacent hypocrisy of the whole spectacle, barbaric and inhuman. One is made to feel that if there is anything Satanic about, it lies in the hearts of the hypocrites and not in the leader of the 'Satanic School'.

The next stanza takes up the hint of some sort of sympathy with the dead king, if only it is the idea that the corpse should be allowed to 'fight/Its way back into earth, and fire, and air'.

Byron even records the king's virtues, though making them seem in keeping with his sweeping the lawn free of dew, for example,

> that household virtue, most uncommon,
> Of constancy to a bad, ugly woman. *xii*

Byron's tongue is very firmly stuck in his cheek, and he can quietly mock the notions of salvation and damnation, as currently purveyed by the doctrine of exclusive salvation for members of the Church of England. Like the devil Byron knows his theology, and he builds up to it with wit and verbal dexterity:

> 'God save the king!' It is a large economy
>   In God to save the like; but if he will
> Be saving, all the better; for not one am I
>   Of those who think damnation better still:
>
> *xiii*

No; it is the ecclesiastical authorities who encourage any contrary notion of damnation. As for himself, goes Byron's irony, he knows that this hope will be unpopular, even blasphemous (leaving confused the notion of Damnation as a notion and the notion of damnation for George III).

> I know my catechism; I know we're cramm'd
>   With the best doctrines till we quite o'erflow;
>   I know that all save England's church have shamm'd,
> And that the other twice two hundred churches
> And synagogues have made a *damn'd* bad purchase.
>
> *xiv*

146

So, by adopting an English voice here, Byron has reduced the theological notion to a height of absurdity (equal in absurdity to the mad king), with a smack at the insular 'British is Best'.

St. Peter is rudely awakened by a parody of Pentecost, 'A rushing sound of wind, and stream, and flame', and a cherub tells him that George the Third is dead; but St. Peter is an obvious non-respecter of persons and is unceremonious in language and behaviour, answering like a bluff, blunt caretaker.

> 'And who *is* George the Third?' replied the Apostle:
> '*What George? what Third?*' 'The king of England,' said
>   The angel. 'Well, he won't find kings to jostle
> Him on his way; but does he wear his head?
>   Because the last we saw here had a tustle,
> And ne'er would have got into heaven's good graces,
> Had he not flung his head in all our faces.
>
> xviii

That was the late King of France, whose head was chopped off by the revolutionary guillotine, and St. Peter would never have let him in at all, but the others were too tender-hearted and overcome by 'fellow-feeling', and he sits in heaven now next to St. Paul ('That fellow Paul—the parvenu'). But the present king arrives, 'an old man/With an old soul, and both extremely blind', and in his wake comes majestic Satan, a superior Giaour:

> His brow was like the deep when tempest-toss'd;
>   Fierce and unfathomable thoughts engraved
> Eternal wrath on his immortal face . . .
>
> xxiv

Fear breaks out in the heavenly company, and even St. Peter

> sweated through his apostolic skin:
>   Of course his perspiration was but ichor,
>   Or some such other spiritual liquor.
>
> xxv

The cherubs form a ring round the king ('for by many stories/ And true, we learn the angels are all Tories'), and then out comes Michael, 'A beautiful and mighty Thing of Light'. There

147

is a splendid meeting of these two antagonists in neutral space, former friends and present foes, but highly civilised both in their behaviour and manners:

> Yet still between his Darkness and his Brightness
> There pass'd a mutual glance of great politeness.

xxxv

Michael is Oriental and bowed 'with a graceful Oriental bend', while Satan

> met his ancient friend
> With more hauteur, as might an old Castilian
> Poor noble meet a mushroom rich civilian.

xxxv

Satan will not beg for the king nor will he shout about his rights and what threats he will utter if the king is not granted to him, but has the tone and language of a great seigneur putting his case mildly and persuasively. He is not, of course, interested in 'Yon weak creation of such paltry things', and he thinks 'few worth damnation but their kings',

> And these but as a king of quit-rent, to
>   Assert my right as lord: and even had
> I such an inclination, 'twere (as you
>   Well know) superfluous; they are grown so bad,
> That hell has nothing better left to do
>   Than leave them to themselves: so much more mad
> And evil by their own internal curse,
> Heaven cannot make them better, nor I worse.

xli

Satan's characterisation of the king is ample and despising as 'this old, blind, mad, helpless, weak, poor worm', and he grants him (like Byron) as much as he can in his favour. He was a tool from the first to last ('I have the workmen safe'), but deserves damnation all the same; he had virtues, but 'tame virtues', as being a 'constant consort', 'decent sire' and 'middling lord'. Nonetheless he oppressed mankind; the opponent of political liberty, and, into the bargain, religious liberty too. You must all, argues Satan, have cold souls

> if you have not abhorr'd
> The foe to Catholic participation
> In all the license of a Christian nation.

xlviii

This persuades St. Peter (the founder of the Catholic Church, as it believes) and he swears not to let this 'royal Bedlam range/ The azure fields of heaven', but Michael interposes and calls for Satan's witnesses.

Here Byron enjoys himself in the manipulation of comparisons between the damned souls and those on earth who have a special privilege to move where they will ('or like to an 'entré'/ Up the back stairs, or such freemasonry') and between the speed of light and 'Satan's couriers'. Solar beams are 'pack'd up for their journey'; the sun's rays pierce the fogs of London and

> The weathercocks are gilt some thrice a year,
> If that the *summer* is not too severe.

lv

Byron is at his most 'Improvisatore' in his management of the verse of the *ottava rima* in stanzas lvii–lviii, fully in his mastering manner:

> Upon the verge of space, about the size
>   Of half-a-crown, a little speck appear'd
> (I've seen a something like it in the skies
>   In the Aegean, ere a squall); it near'd,
> And, growing bigger, took another guise;
>   Like an aerial ship it tack'd, and steer'd
> Or *was* steer'd (I am doubtful of the grammar
> Of the last phrase, which makes the stanza stammer;—
>
> But take your choice): and then it grew a cloud; . . .

His fertility of metaphor springs out in his description of Michael's change of colour when he sees the great host of witnesses brought against the king, a careless and offhand stanza using rhymes just to suit himself and playing a game:

> When Michael saw this host, he first grew pale,
>   As angels can; next, like Italian twilight,

He turn'd all colours—as a peacock's tail,
  Or sunset streaming through a Gothic skylight
In some old abbey, or a trout not stale,
  Or distant lightning on the horizon *by* night,
Or a fresh rainbow, or a grand review
Or thirty regiments in red, green, and blue.

lxi

But Michael is at his most politician-like when he persuades Satan to dismiss this crowd and limit the deposition of testimony to a couple of 'honest, clean/True testimonies' (*lxiii*), because any more will 'stretch our immortality', and, besides,

Our difference is *political*, and I
  Trust that, whatever may occur below
You know my great respect for you: and this
Makes me regret whate'er you do amiss—

lxii

The sight of the two of them talking like this is comic, but we notice the way political differences are managed and this increases the texture of irony in the poem, by making us hear the talk of human party leaders.

Satan allows two witnesses, and they are Wilkes and Junius, Wilkes appearing first. Byron cannot resist a joke wherever he thinks of one, so a comment on Wilkes's old-fashioned clothes leads into the thought that there are all forms of dress in heaven, of all the ages

From Eve's fig-leaf down to the petticoat,
Almost as scanty, of days less remote.

lxvi

The Byron of *The Waltz* is not dead.

Wilkes immediately pretends to think that there must be an election going on to warrant such a press of people and offers himself as candidate 'with unturn'd coat!'

Saint Peter, may I count upon your vote?

lxvii

But his value is not much as a witness for the prosecution, as he will not bring up old scores and turn evidence, and, anyway, Bute and Grafton were the real villains (reinforcing the notion of George III as a tool). Satan treats him as a joker, as he suspected when he saw him whispering near the spit when Belial 'With Fox's lard was basting William Pitt'.

The next witness is Junius, the pseudonymous author of the *Letters of Junius*, a set of letters printed in the late 18th century—the first in 1769—which did much to affect political life at that time in England. They were written in a savagely caustic style, often libellous and always hard-hitting, and, as a 19th-century editor puts it,

> crushed the Duke of Grafton and insulted the Earl of Mansfield; who was a scarecrow of violence to court-jobbers and back-stairs officials, and who conquered the law with his libels.
>
> LETTERS OF JUNIUS

Because his identity was never known for certainty, and a great deal of scholarly argument has raged about the authorship, Byron finds time to digress on the 'phantasmagoria', his features changing so constantly that no one there could recognise him. He presents his own hypothesis, for what it is worth, that there was no *one* person, Junius, at all, nobody at all.

> I don't see wherefore letters should not be
> Written without hands, since we daily view
> Them written without heads; and books, we see,
> Are fill'd without the latter too . . .
>
> *lxxxi*

Junius is not much more forthcoming as a witness than was Wilkes; he says that it is all written in his letters and leaves it at that. He fades away, only to be followed by a commotion as the devil Asmodeus pushes his way to the front of the crowd, carrying Southey the poet. He took him as he was writing what even Asmodeus calls 'a libel/No less on history than the Holy Bible' (*lxxxvi*).

Southey is given his chance to recite his piece, but no one

present wants to hear verse; the poet is stuck fast with the 'gouty feet' of his first hexameter, and the blind mad king speaks his only words:

> 'What! What!
> *Pye* come again? No more—no more of that!'

xcii

The tortured mind remembers the insufferable Poet Laureate, whom thus Byron (unkindly) equates with our new Poet Laureate, Southey.

Michael blows his trumpet for silence and Southey springs not to any defence of the king but to his own, where he (metaphorically) hangs himself. He blows his own trumpet (metaphorically) which he says has 'more of brass in it, and is as well blown' as Michael's. He recites his literary achievements as a turn-coat:

> He had written praises of a regicide;
>   He had written praises of all kings whatever;
> He had written for republics far and wide,
>   And then against them bitterer than ever ...

xcvii

He has written a very great deal of 'blank verse, and blanker prose'; he has written the life of Wesley which qualified him (in his mind) to offer to write the life of Satan, or, when he declines the offer, Michael's life. Satan would have nothing to fear:

> 'Sir, I'm ready to write yours,
> In two octavo volumes, nicely bound,
>   With notes and preface, all that most allures
> The pious purchaser; and there's no ground
>   For fear, for I can choose my own reviewers:
> So let me have the proper documents,
> That I may add you to my other saints.'

xcix

When, at last, he starts his recitation of his 'Vision', the whole 'spiritual show', had vanished 'with variety of scents,/Ambrosial and sulphureous', and it only remained for the impetuous St.

Peter to knock him out of heaven with his keys. He falls from heaven into the lake, but soon comes up to the surface, 'For all corrupted things are buoy'd like corks', and he may be lurking in his den now 'to scrawl some "Life" or "Vision"'.

Meanwhile the old king, forgotten by Southey, ignored by the poem for so long, is seen by the poet in his 'vision' in the final stanza taking advantage of the uproar at heaven's gate over Southey's poetry:

> All I saw further, in the last confusion,
>> Was, that King George slipp'd into heaven for one;
> And when the tumult dwindled to a calm,
> I left him practising the hundredth psalm.

As a satire on politics and religion, as exercises in double-dealing and hypocrisy, Byron's poem is a masterpiece. Its lightness of tone and its sureness of touch, with an impishness and a mocking seriousness as the almost transparent cover for deep indignation and anger, add to a control and good humour which stamps this poem as unique in the language.

To dispose of the king as an unwitting tool, yet despicable in his political role, and, yet again, pitiful and, as a person, harmless, gives added power to the political satire by increasing the complexity of tone within the poem. The deflection of personally scathing poetry on to Southey the renegade is an excellent device to broaden the satire from personal attack on a monarch or on monarchy to an attack both personal and representative, quite a distance from an arraignment of George III (though it is this as well). By a set of accidents, comic or simple, George keeps the place in heaven that Southey would have given him, but one does notice that the patriot witnesses brought against the king are in Satan's keeping and that the angels are Tories. But heaven and hell in the persons of Michael and Satan the aristocrats are extremely well-matched and show a high-minded courtliness, denied, for example, to the rude simplicity of St. Peter, the fisherman.

Attitudes are not simple but sophisticated, but the poem is *fun* to read and makes its 'messages' all the more devastatingly for that.

11

'Don Juan'

Having found his poetic feet in the *ottava rima* of *Beppo* in 1817, Byron constructed his *Don Juan* from 1818 until 1823, the year of his death. This activity was not Byron's only poetic concern during the last years; he wrote most of his drama from 1820 to 1822, and he also wrote *The Vision of Judgment* in 1821.

As well as being modelled on the Italian medley poem, especially as newly seen as a vehicle for English comic writing in Frere's poem (see p. 134), this long work is a complex organism shaped out of all his previous themes and preoccupations, surpassing all his previous literary effort, and becoming peculiarly modern in tone.

Previously he had almost literally projected parts of his own personality and experience into literary forms, what I have brashly called 'fictional biography', and had remained close to rather worn literary conventions (though transcending them at times, it is agreed). The major failing in his previous verse, when compared with his contemporaneous letters, has been a woodenness in style, a rhetorical lift and emphasis in the verse, a stance in the heroes of the grand and eccentric; a presentation of a hero-for-the-times, in competent and often striking verse.

This is an exaggeration, a caricature, but when one comes to *Don Juan* one is so struck by the contrast that caricature of his previous writing is almost inevitable. Now he has a plastic form of which he is master, a form essentially fluent, inevitably pyrotechnic. What he wants to say with this verse now is *everything*. All he has so far written has been a *partial* presentation of what is in Byron the man, in the Byronic imagination, experience and memory. Now he wants to present the whole truth about man and his life, experience and imagination, about man's search for truth, values and reality.

From the evidence one can gather, Byron, having started *Don Juan*, saw that what he had now to do was more than to maintain or safeguard a literary reputation, the reputation of the exciting cavalier of English letters walking his aristocratic and Satanic way through the withdrawing rooms of an England he would never again inhabit, but to tell the truth. His object is to be honest; his target the meretricious and hypocritical; his weapons deflation, comedy, an undercutting and an undermining.

The poem is, in construction, extremely simple. Byron takes a hero and follows him in his adventures from his native Spain as a young man, through his wanderings in exile to the Mediterranean, Turkey, Russia, and to England and his maturity. Basically, then, a picaresque tale in verse. But the hero he seizes is the legendary heartless libertine Don Juan, a man, one might have been tempted to say, after Byron's own heart. At least he is, by definition, some sort of a hero, and Byron admits that, on looking round at possible contemporary figures as potential heroes, he is driven back to 'our ancient friend Don Juan'.

> I want a hero: an uncommon want,
>   When every year and month sends forth a new one,
> Till, after cloying the gazettes with cant,
>   The age discovers he is not the true one:
> Of such as these I should not care to vaunt,
>   I'll therefore take our ancient friend Don Juan—
> We all have seen him, in the pantomime,
> Sent to the devil somewhat ere his time.
>
> I, *i*

However, Byron's Don Juan is not the gentleman of legend, but rather, despite geography and environment, an *English* gentleman, a much-pursued and hunted loved-one, always finding himself willy-nilly involved in amours, never taking the initiative, never predatory and conquering. In fact, someone appears like Byron's own picture of himself. The gentleman-rake is, however, very much present in the poem in the voice of the presenter, Byron, and in the management of commentary, digressions and general presentation. This is the Byron whom only his friends knew in his talk and his talking letters, energetic, sardonic, brilliant and essentially comic. Now the passive agonising of the travelled rhapsodist, Childe Harold, becomes the passive adventures of the naïve Don Juan, guided through his life by a theatrically brilliant satirist, Byron. The previous attempt at the manager–puppet relationship in *Childe Harold* had been leading to this, and he uses the situation again in his drama of 1822, *The Deformed Transformed*.

Whatever Byron's original intentions, and his changing or expanding intentions through the course of writing the poem, it is clear that with a basically picaresque story line he could throw whatever exploits he wished into Don Juan's path if all he were interested in were the variety or multiplicity of amatory adventures. But the fact is, rather, that the poem soon grew into a means of attacking, celebrating and ridiculing in verse anything that Byron thought worth his energy. In this way, *Don Juan* is much closer to the original notion of satire as a medley, the Horatian satire as a poem essentially loose in construction and mingling all the interests of the writer, and it is little wonder that one of the epigraphs for the poem was Horace's '*Difficile est proprie communia dicere*' ('It's hard to give perfect expression to familiar thoughts'). We see, too, that though Byron is no longer writing in Popean couplets and aligning himself in that way with the poetry of social man, he is still concerned with poetry as a means of examining *man* in this rather old-fashioned idiom.

But simply to see the poem as another example of 'The proper study of mankind is man' is unfair to it. Byron wants us to recognise it as an *epic* poem, a poem of the highest seriousness, according to the canons of literature inherited by the Western World from its classical progenitors. And yet this recognition is an ironic recognition that this poem is *not* an epic, and Byron has his tongue firmly in his cheek, playing with our expectations and our newness to his essentially wandering and digressive manner. Having given in I, *vi* the injunction that Horace gave to epic poets to 'plunge "*in medias res*"', he goes on:

That is the usual method, but not mine—
　My way is to begin with the beginning;
The regularity of my design
　Forbids all wandering as the worst of sinning,
And therefore I shall open with a line
　(Although it cost me half an hour in spinning)
Narrating somewhat of Don Juan's father,
And also of his mother, if you'd rather.

I, vii

This marriage of ease and graceful mockery, the quite obvious
falsity of saying that a line could cost such a manipulator of
verse 'half an hour in spinning' when the parenthesis is itself a
piece of panache and cunning, the refusal to keep to a straight
line while digressing to say that digression 'is the worst of
sinning', all point to those qualities which lift *Don Juan* into
greatness. What one notices also is the way that this sort of
writing could quite simply become anarchic, with no organisation, no line to hold on to, no values, a total abnegation of all
positives for the uncomfortable bleakness of positive cancelled
by negative. What keeps the poem together, more than the slim
narrative line of events in the life of the hero, is the magnificent
manner of the poet and his own puzzlement at the world and its
values, and at man's essential absurdity.

Byron in *Don Juan* is a new literary personality, if one has in
mind those other personalities which Byron's public would have
experienced. But, in a real sense, Byron is catching up again into
this poem all that he has achieved in literature as the Romance
writer, as the Sentimentalist, as the Myth-creator of modern
Europe, as the presenter of the descriptive and emotionally
moving tour. He said, for what it is worth, that he had meant
to make Don Juan

> a *Cavaliere Servente* in Italy, and a cause for a divorce in England,
> and a Sentimental 'Werther-faced man' in Germany, so as to show
> the different ridicules of the Society in those countries.

But his concern was not simply with presenting an *alter ego*, following roughly the pattern of his own existence and experiences, in order to satirise the various societies Don Juan (Byron) happened to find himself living with. His concern was broader than this; to satirise that which struck Byron as ridiculous in everything, including Juan himself; to recognise a new role, the satirist as buffoon, as court jester. Something of this must be recognised before we can see exactly why Byron chooses to deal with certain issues, to attack certain institutions and people, including himself.

Cynicism could be said to be a mockery, a cold, heartless mockery of values held, or ostensibly held, by others, and Byron is not simply mocking. He is, indeed, gleeful in his attack on 'cant', on hypocrisy, on two-faced politicians, but there is a recognition by Byron of humanity, what Wordsworth called 'the still, sad music of humanity' (*Tintern Abbey*). The deflating mockery and exposure of cant goes side by side with a willing recognition on Byron's part that to attack individuals, ideas or institutions demands, rightly, that one has something by which one judges these people and things and by which one could replace them. But Byron has very little dogma to offer, very little certainty, very little faith; and yet he can recognise dishonesty. Honesty of response, if only an honest scepticism, is the only admirable mode of conducting oneself.

So Byron spoke his mind, and, if his speech was to be honest, it had to be spoken as he would speak it, even deliberately in defiance of the 'half-and-half' prudery of contemporary England, even if it meant shouting insults at men like Castlereagh, the 'intellectual eunuch' (I, *xi*).

Speaking his mind entailed voicing his prejudices, social, literary, political and moral, and attacking the objects of his hatred and disgust anywhere he found, or planted, them. He 'dedicated' his poem to Southey, now abhorrent to Byron as a turncoat who once had written for Liberty against Tyranny, now a softened and obedient slave, even Tyranny's official Poet Laureate.

BOB SOUTHEY! You're a poet—Poet-laureate,
    And representative of all the race;

Although 'tis true that you turn'd out a Tory at
    Last,—yours has lately been a common case;
And now, my Epic Renegade! what are ye at?
    With all the Lakers, in and out of place?
A nest of tuneful persons, to my eye
Like 'four and twenty Blackbirds in a pye';

Dedication, i

His response to Southey is mocking, and even scurrilous, as when in the third stanza he turns the dominant metaphor from bird to fish:

And then you overstrain yourself, or so,
    And tumble downward like the flying fish
Gasping on deck, because you soar too high, Bob,
And fall, for lack of moisture quite a-dry, Bob!

Dedication, iii

The entry in Partridge's *Dictionary of Slang* gives the definition of a 'dry bob' as 'coition without male emission', and Southey joins the later figure of attack, Castlereagh, as an 'intellectual eunuch'.

It was only to be expected that this sort of writing would cause consternation, giving grave offence to living individuals and to the sensibilities of the reading public in England; in fact, it screamed libel. Furore there was, though *Cain* in 1821 raised more, but there was enough in the writing to give Murray, Byron's publisher, anxiety and heartburn.

The young Don Juan shares several of the young Byron's experiences, though this time there is an older, worldly-wise and witty Byron present to act as commentator. So, English educational tinkerings with the classics, expurgation, is one incidental butt for Byron's amusement:

Juan was taught from out the best edition,
    Expurgated by learned men, who place,
Judiciously, from out the schoolboy's vision,
    The grosser parts; but, fearful to deface
Too much their modest bard by this omission,
    And pitying sore this mutilated case,

They only add them all in an appendix,
Which saves, in fact, the trouble of an index;

I, xliv

While this jokes against Byron's own experiences at Harrow, no doubt, we have a building up of the way Don Juan sees sensuality everywhere, the young adolescent no less. So, the innocent sixteen-year-old meets and falls for a married and experienced woman, Donna Julia, at the ripe age of twenty-three:

These few short years make wondrous alterations,
Particularly amongst sun-burnt nations.

I, lxix

Now Byron has the really admirable case for a demonstration telling against the false language of literary passion, its sentimentality, that is, its falsity. The sighs, tender glances, and so on, 'tremblings when met, and restlessness when left', are all there, as one might imagine that they would be, and Byron gives them full play in one stanza. They are all 'little preludes to possession',

Of which young passions cannot be bereft,

(but the concluding couplet throws all into confusion, shrivels up the magic and frailty of young love)

And merely tend to show how greatly love is
Embarrass'd at first starting with a novice.

I, lxxiv

And so, true to fashion and literature, the young man seeks the open country to solace his aching heart and to commune with nature. (And here one thinks of Tom Jones and his meeting with Molly Seagrim whilst he is in full spate of a sentimental invocation of his adored—but distant—Sophia.) Juan's mind soars splendidly, and Byron allows the verse to float easily upwards, elastically, for one stanza, to mirror his 'metaphysical state', as Byron imagines Coleridge would, and then sets Byronic reflection alongside this 'Wordsworthian' musing:

He thought about himself, and the whole earth,
  Of man the wonderful, and of the stars,
And how the deuce they ever could have birth;
  And then he thought of earthquakes, and of wars,
How many miles the moon might have in girth,
  Of air-balloons, and of the many bars
To perfect knowledge of the boundless skies;—
And then he thought of Donna Julia's eyes.

I, xcii

And in the following stanza, cannily echoing certain phrases of
Wordsworth's, Byron brings down all the air-blown metaphysics to physical bed-rock:

In thoughts like these true wisdom may discern
  Longings sublime and aspirations high,
Which some are born with, but the most part learn
  To plague themselves withal, they know not why:
'Twas strange that one so young should thus concern
  His brain about the action of the sky;
If *you* think 'twas philosophy that this did,
I can't help thinking puberty assisted.

I, xciii

The primary fact in the case, physiology, is the one aspect of
the situation which would not have been adverted to in a *literary*
presentation of love, and this is what Byron is really mocking.

Physiology plays its part in the little drama all right, and the
continued meeting of Juan and Donna Julia issues in the
inevitable:

A little still she strove, and much repented,
And whispering 'I will ne'er consent'—consented.

I, cxvii

The husband returns to burst into the bedroom to catch, one
imagines, the guilty pair *in flagrante delicto*. But he finds no man
and we, the audience, find injustice well done. Julia turns out
to be a consummate actress, playing the part of an outraged
innocent wife (though only someone more than naïve could
find the things to say that she does). Rhetorical questions like

hailstones pour down on Don Alfonzo's head, berating him, jeering at him, mocking at him and reviling him. This is splendid theatre and shows Byron's real theatrical skill. When the baffled husband leaves and the door is bolted, Byron puts on a parallel mock-serious display:

> No sooner was it bolted, than—Oh shame!
>   Oh sin! Oh sorrow! and Oh womankind!
> How can you do such things and keep your fame,
>   Unless this world, and t'other too, be blind?
> Nothing so dear as an unfilch'd good name!
>   But to proceed—for there is more behind:
> With much heartfelt reluctance be it said,
> Young Juan slipp'd, half-smother'd, from the bed.
>
> I, clxv

And the mock-serious condemnation takes in Juan himself; he is beyond our sympathy now, the mockery runs:

> He had no business to commit a sin,
> Forbid by heavenly, fined by human laws;
>   At least 'twas rather early to begin;
>
> I, clxvii

But Don Alfonzo discovers Juan's shoes in the bedroom, and amid hand-to-hand fighting, hysterics, clamour and confusion, Juan escapes, leaving his last piece of clothing in Alfonzo's hand. Juan is shipped off to Cadiz by his mother and Donna Julia is sent to a convent. Julia writes Juan a letter which sounds as fervid and overheated as did Lady Caroline Lamb's letters to Byron. Donna Inez, incidentally, as Juan's mother, has traits of Byron's wife, having her 'favourite science' the 'Mathematical', and a coldness of heart with a corresponding strict propriety and prissiness which Byron presents as abhorrent:

> Oh! she was perfect past all parallel—
>   Of any modern female saint's comparison;
> So far above the cunning powers of hell,
>   Her guardian angel had given up his garrison;
> Even her minutest motions went as well
>   As those of the best time-piece made by Harrison:

In virtues nothing earthly could surpass her,
Save thine 'incomparable oil', Macassar!

I, xvii

But she and all the *dramatis personae* are held in abeyance while
the canto ends with some reflections by Byron on his 'modern
epic' and his theoretic plans and the reader's expectations. All is
mocked: the dogmatic critic who works by rules and prescrip-
tions; the morality-monger who wants literature to contain trite
moral saws dressed out; the mighty Critical Journals with their
power to make or break a writer; all are reviewed and knocked
down. Byron is now taking stock of himself and recognising the
need he has to write what *he must write*. His life is ebbing:

I

Have spent my life, both interest and principal,
And deem not, what I deem'd, my soul invincible.

I, ccxiii

He reviews his life in a comically soured way and finds that he
cannot write for glory now; he recognises the old theme of *Childe
Harold's Pilgrimage* of the fleetingness of man and his history,
but this time he expresses the thought with an unsentimental
daring, a comedy and a wryness that is delightful.

What are the hopes of man? Old Egypt's King
   Cheops erected the first pyramid
And largest, thinking it was just the thing
   To keep his memory whole, and mummy hid:
But somebody or other rummaging,
   Burglariously broke his coffin's lid:
Let not a monument give you or me hopes,
Since not a pinch of dust remains of Cheops.

I, ccxix

Childe Harold's come home again; the grandiloquent language
and theatrical gesturing are tempered by burlesque and mockery.

Just as Byron takes his earlier grand themes and redirects them,
so Juan's own sentimentality meets reality head on and stands
abashed and foolish. When, in Canto II, Juan is aboard ship

leaving his native Seville for Cadiz and is preparing a moving speech of farewell to his native country and his Julia, clutching his Caroline Lambish letter, his simple and single-minded sentimentality meets the swell of the sea:

> And oh! if e'er I should forget, I swear—
>   But that's impossible, and cannot be—
> Sooner shall this blue ocean melt to air,
>   Sooner shall earth resolve itself to sea,
> Than I resign thine image, oh, my fair!
>   Or think of anything, excepting thee;
> A mind diseased no remedy can physic—
>   (Here the ship gave a lurch, and he grew sea-sick.)
>
> Sooner shall heaven kiss earth—(here he fell sicker)
>   Oh, Julia! what is every other woe?—
> (For God's sake let me have a glass of liquor;
>   Pedro, Battista, help me down below.)
> Julia, my love—(you rascal, Pedro, quicker)
>   Oh, Julia!—(this curst vessel pitches so)—
> Beloved Julia, hear me still beseeching!'
> (Here he grew inarticulate with retching.)

> II, *xix–xx*

This reduces Don Juan to the common condition of man, and destroys his theatrical (i.e. false) leavetaking, and, indeed, echoes Byron's own stanzas on leaving England in 1809. And, having reduced his hero to the level of man at the mercy of events, absurdly living on one level of sentimental attachment of mind and heart, while being necessarily subject to the physiological machine of his body, Byron allows himself some general reflection on Love. He had, in Canto I, deliberately reduced love to the physiological, and here he presents a different and amused, though realistic, view of human passion:

> Love's a capricious power: I've known it hold
>   Out through a fever caused by its own heat,
> But be much puzzled by a cough and cold,
>   And find a quinzy very hard to treat;
> Against all noble maladies he's bold,

> But vulgar illnesses don't like to meet,
> Nor that a sneeze should interrupt his sigh,
> Nor inflammations redden his blind eye.

II, xxii

Byron speaks out of a lifetime of experience, and it seems as though his autobiography is being written in this poem. So, when the ship springs a leak and all the masts have to be cut away to right the foundering ship, Byron slips into using 'we' (II, *xxxii*) almost automatically. He speaks in this stanza of 'our intent', and says 'Although we never meant/To part with all till every hope was blighted'; and we remind ourselves of how Byron always turned to facts for the basis of his writing whenever possible. However, nothing in this poem is simple; autobiography is one element in a total review of man and man's life.

The set-piece of heroic writing, the storm and shipwreck, the doomed struggle of brave men against the raging elements, becomes the serio-comic business of the poet seeing life whole. The sailors get drunk, and Juan's valet, Pedro, jumped drunkenly to his death: 'And so he found a wine-and-watery grave' (II, *lvii*). The sailors try to throw as much food and drink into the boat as they can—and itemised by Quartermaster Byron exactly, a curiously reductive technique—and they are left at the mercy of the elements. Food and drink soon run out and cannibalism is the only way to survive. 'Gothic comedy' is, I suppose, the only expression for what follows in Byron's treatment of the situation. He allows us to realise the horror of cannibalism and then uses his verse-handling to introduce a frivolity and levity which is the source of the macabre comedy. (Though, perhaps, one ought to make the point that Byron is old-fashioned and aristocratic enough to have his hero refuse human meat, and so escape going mad—the retribution taken on the others in the boat.) The couplet of each of three stanzas (II, *lxxv, lxxvii, lxxviii*) bumps us down to a startled recognition of bathos in a scene of such strongly emotive content. When lots have been cast for the first of the crew to be eaten, no one was to blame, says Byron:

'Twas Nature gnaw'd them to this resolution,
By which none were permitted to be neuter—
And the lot fell on Juan's luckless tutor.

II, lxxv

When the surgeon had done his work of butchery and Pedrillo had been koshered,

> Part was divided, part thrown in the sea,
>   And such things as the entrails and the brains
> Regaled two sharks, who follow'd o'er the billow—
> The sailors ate the rest of poor Pedrillo.

II, lxxvii

The music-hall clowning of the last line where the sentiments go with a dancing flirting on to its feminine rhyme is a very good example of the deflationary method as used in rhyme and rhythm, but, more than that, the reader's attention is focused on the absurdity of the situation rather than on its horrific bestiality. Even Juan's refusal to eat human meat is put into non-heroic terms, as far as possible, and jokes are needed by Byron:

> 'Twas not to be expected that he should,
> Even in extremity of their disaster,
> Dine with them on his pastor and his master.

II, lxxviii

Having made that clear, and having appreciated something of Byron's knockdown verse, we must recognise that he can still be as sentimental as ever himself. So, the same canto shows two fathers with sons aboard the fated boat, a situation with a gilt-edged guarantee of sentimentality as the sons weaken and die inevitably, and Byron rises to his own bait in verse like:

> And o'er him bent his sire, and never raised
>   His eyes from off his face, but wiped the foam
> From his pale lips, and ever on him gazed,
>   And when the wish'd-for shower at length was come,
> And the boy's eyes, which the dull film half glazed,
>   Brighten'd, and for a moment seem'd to roam,

He squeezed from out a rag some drops of rain
Into his dying child's mouth—but in vain.

II, *lxxxix*

One looks in vain for the explosive landmine in the couplet, and, though one might approve both motive, deed and exhibition of selfless love, one must say that Byron's verse is wooden, unmoving and banal. In a larger sense, though, one recognises this sort of thing as only another indication of the rapid shuttle from pole to pole of literary experience that Byron makes his reader perform in the reading of this poem. And this sort of sentimentality should warn us about the desert island where Don Juan, the sole survivor of the shipwreck, finally lands.

True to a forecast, possibly, the island is a miniature paradise, with an unfallen, virginal, unEnglish dream-Eve. The presenter, Byron, keeps us amused by his worldly-wise sallies and divagations, having fun with the thought of the beautiful Haidee's piratical father, human misfortunes in general, and his own habits of sleeping by day and working by night, but Haidee comes off unscathed. She is all heroine, all beauty, all care, all devotion, all passion; nothing can modify Byron's (and our) view of her. Of course, Byron will not let us *simply* escape into a world where the commonplace no longer has meaning; he keeps the balloon of romance tethered, albeit lightly, to the ground. Zoe, the maidservant, is a sort of practical Sancho Panza when the imagination and the emotions are engaged on Haidee's side. While Haidee is acting true to romance, Zoe is bringing us down to base again:

And thus like to an angel o'er the dying
　　Who die in righteousness, she lean'd; and there
All tranquilly the shipwreck'd boy was lying,
　　As o'er him lay the calm and stirless air:
But Zoe the meantime some eggs was frying,
　　Since, after all, no doubt the youthful pair
Must breakfast, and betimes—lest they should ask it,
She drew out her provision from the basket.

II, *cxliv*

And Juan himself, though an ideal object for ideal love, young and handsome, does not escape fully Byron's restraining hand:

> In short, he was a very pretty fellow,
> Although his woes had turn'd him rather yellow.
>
> II, cxlviii

But, an idyll it is, nonetheless, and it remains Byron's tribute to Sentimental Love, perhaps all the more remarkable from its framing context in the large-scale masterful mockery and serious playfulness of the poem as a whole. Haidee is treated so gently and so lightly that she remains memorable in the gamut of Byron's heroines. Byron seems to recognise the incident as a sort of intoxication for him, an escape from sober reality, and he embeds some thoughts on drunkenness in his treatment of the idyll, sandwiched between a description of the coastal scenery seen by the lovers on their island paradise.

> Man, being reasonable, must get drunk;
>   The best of life is but intoxication:
> Glory, the grape, love, gold, in these are sunk
>   The hopes of all men, and of every nation;
> Without their sap, how branchless were the trunk
>   Of life's strange tree, so fruitful on occasion!
> But to return,—Get very drunk; and when
> You wake with headache, you shall see what then.
>
> II, clxxix

After drunkenness the reckoning; and all love is fatal to the lover; and Byron spends the first eleven stanzas of Canto III sadly reflecting on human love and its fraility. His reflections lead him inevitably into the state of matrimony, and here he is witty, if not also wise:

> 'Tis melancholy, and a fearful sign
>   Of human frailty, folly, also crime,
> That love and marriage rarely can combine,
>   Although they both are born in the same clime;
> Marriage from love, like vinegar from wine—
>   A sad, sour, sober beverage—by time

Is sharpen'd from its high celestial flavour,
Down to a very homely household savour.

III, v

Byron's attention now focuses with real enjoyment on the
returning pirate, Lambro, Haidee's father, for whom Byron has
an obvious sympathy. How could he not after his own series of
devil-may-care piratical heroes of the Romances? Something of
Byron's own experience of the Pashas he met on his first journey
is around in the mild manners and ruthless behaviour of Lambro:

... He was the mildest manner'd man
  That ever scuttled ship or cut a throat,
With such true breeding of a gentleman,
  You never could divine his real thought;
No courtier could, and scarcely woman can
  Gird more deceit within a petticoat;
Pity he loved adventurous life's variety,
He was so great a loss to good society.

III, xli

And Lambro, instead of being the father returning, having been
reported dead, now to be outraged at his daughter's behaviour,
and the simple instrument to get Juan from this adventure to the
next (as the outraged husband had been in Canto I), is treated
fully enough to have a history, a psychology and a personality.
He is essentially Greek, and is reacting against the degradation of
his country, and Byron's own Grecian experiences are involved
in this canto.

Byron's shaping imagination is so eclectic and unfussy that it
can include in this canto (with an awkward transition) the lyric
poem *The Isles of Greece*. This was a poem which he had written
previously but which was still unpublished. It really belongs to
Childe Harold's Pilgrimage, having no undercutting ironies, but is
a simple and heartfelt cry for the past glory of Greece and its
present state of slavery, moving in a strong and compelling
rhythmic order. The first stanza gives some idea of the general
quality of the lyric:

The isles of Greece, the isles of Greece!
  Where burning Sappho loved and sung,
Where grew the arts of war and peace,
  Where Delos rose, and Phoebus sprung!
Eternal summer gilds them yet,
But all, except their sun, is set.

III, lxxxvi

This song leads Byron, almost inevitably, being Byron, into a long reflection for the rest of the canto on poets and poetry. He both wilfully and knowingly flaunts his digressive manner before the reader, and all attempts to pull his story together fail magnificently. As soon as he remembers his theme off he goes again:

But let me to my story: I must own,
  If I have any fault, it is digression,
Leaving my people to proceed alone,
  While I soliloquize beyond expression:
But these are my addresses from the throne,
  Which put off business to the ensuing session:
Forgetting each omission is a loss to
The world, not quite so great as Ariosto.

III, xcvi

And so he's slipped away again for another four stanzas on Southey, Horace, Wordsworth and Dryden, and when he comes, digressively again, to the close of the stanza he mocks the reader and the critic by letting his cobbling method come confidentially out:

I feel this tediousness will never do—
  'Tis being *too* epic, and I must cut down
(In copying), this long canto into two;
  They'll never find it out, unless I own
The fact, excepting some experienced few;
  And then as an improvement 'twill be shown:
I'll prove that such the opinion of the critic is
From Aristotle *passim*.—See Ποιητικης.

III, cxi

The fourth canto sees the inevitable wounding of Juan by Lambro and Haidee's tragic death, the close of the idyll; but at the opening of the canto Byron lets his cynical guard slip:

> And if I laugh at any mortal thing,
>   'Tis that I may not weep; and if I weep,
> 'Tis that our nature cannot always bring
>   Itself to apathy, for we must steep
> Our hearts first in the depths of Lethe's spring,
>   Ere what we least wish to behold will sleep:
> Thetis baptized her mortal son in Styx;
> A mortal mother would on Lethe fix.
>
> <div align="right">IV, <i>iv</i></div>

This sort of statement, one feels, comes very close to Byron's inner response to life and its jocoseriousness, and it certainly qualifies one's attitude to the Byron of *Don Juan*. But Byron slips easily into the predictable responses when he comes to Haidee's death which is the occasion for sentimental lament, and all the organ stops are out for the voluntary:

> She died, but not alone; she held within
>   A second principle of life, which might
> Have dawn'd a fair and sinless child of sin;
>   But closed its little being without light,
> And went down to the grave unborn, wherein
>   Blossom and bough lie wither'd with one blight;
> In vain the dews of Heaven descend above
> The bleeding flower and blasted fruit of love.
>
> <div align="right">IV, <i>lxx</i></div>

But what one could never have predicted was the following stanza, a sombre and lyrically splendid stanza, vowel-savouring and fine-cadenced, one of the best short emotional pieces of Byron's whole works:

> That isle is now all desolate and bare,
>   Its dwellings down, its tenants pass'd away;
> None but her own and father's grave is there,
>   And nothing outward tells of human clay;
> Ye could not know where lies a thing so fair,
>   No stone is there to show, no tongue to say,

> What was; no dirge, except the hollow sea's,
> Mourns o'er the beauty of the Cyclades.
>
> <div align="right">IV, <i>lxxii</i></div>

A whole world of regret lies in the stanza, a lament for the passing of Byron's most memorable love-situation, a lament for and celebration of Byron's own ideal Greece.

Juan is shipped as a slave for the Turkish slave markets, and Byron introduces us to a party of opera singers as Juan's companions for the market through the account given of them by the 'buffo' of the party. This is entertaining, nothing to do with the story, and a picaresque sort of incident, whose only justification for appearing at all is just that Byron happened to be thinking about opera in terms of green-room envy and detraction. But one admits Byron's liveliness and 'truth':

> The tenor's voice is spoilt by affectation,
>   And for the bass, the beast can only bellow;
> In fact, he had no singing education,
>   An ignorant, noteless, timeless, tuneless fellow;
> But being the prima-donna's near relation,
>   Who swore his voice was very rich and mellow,
> They hired him, though to hear him you'd believe
> An ass was practising recitative.
>
> <div align="right">IV, <i>lxxxvii</i></div>

In Canto V, at the slave sale, Juan is placed next to a typical Englishman (by Fate and Byron). He has Byron's virtues of sang-froid, stiff upper lip and quiet courage, and Byron catches him acutely and with insight through his speech:

> 'My boy!'—said he, 'amidst this motley crew
>   Of Georgians, Russians, Nubians, and what not,
> All ragamuffins differing but in hue,
>   With whom it is our luck to cast our lot,
> The only gentlemen seem I and you;
>   So let us be acquainted, as we ought:
> If I could yield you any consolation,
> 'Twould give me pleasure.—Pray, what is your nation?'
>
> <div align="right">V, <i>xiii</i></div>

His reply to Juan's questioning is superb:

'Pray, sir' said Juan, 'if I may presume,
   What brought you here?'—'Oh! nothing very rare—
Six Tartars and a drag-chain—'

V, xv

In the midst of the buying and selling of the slave market Byron
has his usual digression, but this time he digresses within the
digression to incorporate a recent personal experience, covering
seven stanzas, of his finding the military commandant in Ravenna
shot in the street. He wrote a prose account of the incident in a
letter to Murray of 9 December 1820, the evening of the incident.
The verse and prose accounts are substantially identical. The
incident itself was a demonstration of Byron's courage and
humanity, as the man was, of course, a representative of the
regime the populace (and Byron) hated. As Byron says in his
letter:

> It seems that, if I had not taken him into my house, he might have
> lain in the Streets till morning; as nobody meddles with such
> things, for fear of the Consequences—either of public suspicion or
> private revenge on the part of the Slayers. They may do as they
> please: I shall never be deterred from a duty of humanity by all
> the assassins of Italy, and that is a wide word.

And so the poem progresses, taking Juan into a harem disguised
as a woman, an object of sexual desire on all sides, from the
harem to the siege of Ismael on the Danube, fighting for the
Russians against the Turks, from the Danube to the Imperial
court of Catherine the Great, and from thence to England. Constantly Juan is involved, willy-nilly, with fortune, war and
women, and he remains the passive tool in the hands of fate
and his creator. More and more as Byron's poem progresses,
and his poetic hand is in, do we see Byron's preoccupations with
the lack of certainty in life and the corresponding lack of fixed
and invariable values. We see, too, Byron's own anguish under-
cut by his own irony, by his verse-form and by his manipulation
of the *ottava rima*. He recognises his own verse for what it is and
gives the best description of it at the opening of Canto VII:

O Love! O Glory! what are you who fly
    Around us ever, rarely to alight?
There's not a meteor in the Polar sky
    Of such transcendent and more fleeting flight.
Chill, and chain'd to cold earth, we lift on high
    Our eyes in search of either lovely light;
A thousand and a thousand colours they
Assume, then leave us on our freezing way.

And such as they are, such my present tale is,
    A nondescript and ever-varying rhyme,
A versified Aurora Borealis,
    Which flashes o'er a waste and icy clime.
When we know what all are, we must bewail us,
    But ne'ertheless I hope it is no crime
To laugh at *all* things—for I wish to know
What, after *all*, are *all* things—but a *show*?

VII, *i, ii*

Byron sees himself as the great entertainer, reducing the old
pieties and old certainties of the classical writer of epic to a
modern scepticism, sardonic, mocking, deliberately self-
defeating. The old ways of Homer's celebrating the glorious
combat of heroes and their magnificent fighting and dying are
seen, by Byron, over against the modern experiences of war, the
futility and waste, the horror and maiming of men and property,
though in a society which still retains the continuing absurdities
of 'Medals, ranks, ribands, lace, embroidery, scarlet' (V, *lxxxiv*).
This rouses him to heights of savage scorn and indignation against
all war and its 'agonies and crimes' (VIII, *cxxv*), and he has a
biting parody of the patriot's cry of 'God save the King':

But still there is unto a patriot nation,
    Which loves so well its country and its king,
A subject of sublimest exultation—
    Bear it, ye Muses, on your brightest wing!
Howe'er the mighty locust, Desolation
    Strip your green fields, and to your harvest cling,
Gaunt famine never shall approach the throne—
Though Ireland starve, great George weighs twenty stone.

VIII, *cxxvi*

174

And, in a phrase, 'War's a brain-spattering, windpipe-slitting art' (IX, *iv*).

Death and the thoughts of death only bring Byron to an abyss, dark and bottomless, of uncertainty:

> There's no such thing as certainty, that's plain
>> As any of Mortality's conditions;
> So little do we know what we're about in
> This world, I doubt if doubt itself be doubting.
>
> IX, xvii

Life, too, is a curio, an oddity, an absurdity ('What a curious way/The whole thing is of clothing souls in clay!' (IX, *lxxv*)), and love, the irrational, is as good a means of ordering an absurd universe as the madness of verse is for ordering the reflection of that absurd existence:

> Besides Platonic love, besides the love
>> Of God, the love of sentiment, the loving
> Of faithful pairs—(I needs must rhyme with dove,
>> That good old steam-boat which keeps verses moving
> 'Gainst reason—Reason ne'er was hand-and-glove
>> With rhyme, but always leant less to improving
> The sound than sense) besides all these pretences
> To love, there are those things which words name senses;
>
> IX, lxxiv

The correct response to Catherine the Great's lust for Juan is, for Byron, an amused and tolerant smile at human folly and curiosity, and, when Juan's mother refuses to recognise the situation for what it is and sends a hypocritical letter to her son, Byron sings out:

> Oh for a *forty-parson power* to chant
> Thy praise, Hypocrisy!
>
> X, xxxiv

And English Hypocrisy is the main game for the rest of the existing poem, and the England that Byron had known as a Regency dandy and lionised poet is the object of this satire. There are some magnificent stanzas, but they are much more embedded in rather casual and quiet conversation in this last part of the poem, much more so than has been the case in the earlier part. The general manner is more assured, and the spectacular displays in verse have tended to seep away; but splendours are there. The coquette, for example, is pinned quivering to the dissection board:

> Such is your cold coquette, who can't say 'No,'
>   And won't say 'Yes,' and keeps you on and off-ing
> On a lee-shore, till it begins to blow—
>   Then sees your heart wreck'd with an inward scoffing.
> This works a world of sentimental woe,
>   And sends new Werters yearly to their coffin;
> But yet is merely innocent flirtation.
> Not quite adultery, but adulteration.

XII, lxiii

All in all we must recognise that Byron has achieved one of the finest comic poems in our language in *Don Juan*, running the whole range of the spectrum from the mordant and maliciously sardonic to the gaiety and polish of a sprightly wit. It has a quality of greatness because it has a seriousness behind the humour, the agony of doubt and of the absurd, the recognition of the inextricable tangle of the noble and the disgusting in what we know as human life.

Postscript: Byronism

'L'astre étrange vers lequel va graviter tout notre Romantisme.'

Any handbook* on European Romanticism in the 19th century will show the English reader one remarkable fact: Byron was a heroic model for all literary aspirants. In France Musset and Mérimée imitated the Byronic stance of the great aristocrat writing verse to alleviate boredom, and young writers after 1830 drank from skulls and engaged in orgies which they imagined were like those of Byron at Newstead. They became, in their imaginations, those oriental heroes with blasted and ravaged face, as one sees in Gautier's *L'Histoire du Romantisme*, at the same time as they fell under the spell of Sir Walter Scott's Middle Ages, and letters were full of startling passions and a gust for crime which became recognisably 'byronisme'.

Byron was the dominant influence; it was his assertion of the individual against all established values which ushered in the Romantic revolution, and his voice spoke loudly and convincingly throughout Europe.

A final word. His name is still a magic name, and a story is told of an official celebration recently held for a minor Russian poet of whom all that the toast makers at the banquet could say was that his poetry was 'full of sunny optimism'. An aged peasant poet, sitting near the guest of honour, turned and asked if he had heard of Lord Byron. He was, said the old to the younger poet, a great English lord, exceedingly rich and the handsomest man in all Europe. The ladies flocked round him, and he was the envy of the world. His poetry was pessimistic, so what did the Russian poet have to be optimistic about?

* E.g. Louis Reynaud, *La Romantisme: Les Origines Anglo-Germaniques*, Paris, 1926.

Bibliography

BIOGRAPHY

The standard biography is now Leslie A. Marchand, *Byron, A Biography*, 3 vols. (Alfred A. Knopf, Inc., New York, 1957).

GENERAL CRITICAL WORKS

Edward E. Bostetter, *The Romantic Ventriloquists* (Univ. of Wash. Press, Seattle, Wash., 1963).

Robert F. Gleckner, *Byron and the Ruins of Paradise* (Johns Hopkins Press, Baltimore, Md., 1967).

Leslie A. Marchand, *Byron's Poetry: A Critical Introduction* (Harvard Univ. Press, Cambridge, Mass., 1965).

Andrew Rutherford, *Byron: A Critical Study* (Stanford University Press, Stanford, Calif., 1961).

LETTERS AND JOURNALS

Byron: A Self-Portrait, ed. Peter Quennell, 2 vols. (Humanities Press, Inc., New York, 1950).

Life, Letters and Journals of Lord Byron, ed. Moore, Thomas (Reprint House International, New York, 1901).

Lord Byron's Correspondence (Dufour Editions Inc., Chester Springs, Pa., 1922).

"CHILDE HAROLD'S PILGRIMAGE"

Ernest J. Lowell, Jr., *Byron: The Record of a Quest* (Univ. of Texas Press, Austin, Tex., 1949).

Harold Bloom, *The Visionary Company: A Reading of English Romantic Poetry* (Anchor Doubleday, New York).

Allan Rodway, *The Romantic Conflict* (Humanities Press Inc., New York, 1950).

BYRON'S SATIRE

Claude M. Fuess, *Lord Byron as a Satirist in Verse* (Haskell House, New York, 1912, reissued 1964).

F. R. Leavis, "Byron's Satire" in *Revaluation* (W. W. Norton & Co., Inc., New York, 1963).

BYRON'S DRAMA

Samuel C. Chew, Jr., *The Drama of Lord Byron: A Critical Study* (Russell & Russell, New York, 1915, reissued 1964).

"DON JUAN"

C. M. Bowra, *Romantic Imagination* (Oxford Univ. Press, New York, 1961).

Elizabeth F. Boyd, *Don Juan, A Critical Study* (Humanities Press Inc., New York).

George M. Ridenour, *The Style of Don Juan* (Yale Univ. Press, New Haven, Conn., 1960).

BYRONISM

Bertrand Russell, *History of Western Philosophy*, Chap. XXIII (Simon and Schuster, New York, 1959).

Index

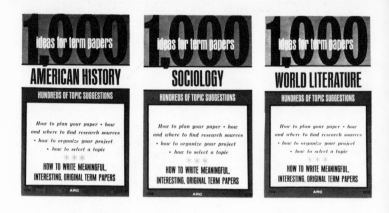

Get More Mileage Out of Your Study Time!
ARCO NOTES

An all-new series of study aids to help you get better grades in your lit courses. Each book gives chapter-by-chapter summaries, a brief general summary of the work, sketches of all major characters, a brief biography of the author, and an essential annotated bibliography. Use **Arco Notes**—they stick in your memory! 95¢ each

THE AENEID
CRIME AND PUNISHMENT
DAVID COPPERFIELD
THE DIVINE COMEDY
GREAT EXPECTATIONS
HAMLET
THE HOUSE OF THE SEVEN GABLES
HUCKLEBERRY FINN
THE ILIAD
IVANHOE
JANE EYRE
JULIUS CAESAR
LEAVES OF GRASS
LORD JIM
MACBETH

MAN AND SUPERMAN
THE MERCHANT OF VENICE
MOBY DICK
MY ANTONIA
THE ODYSSEY
OTHELLO
PRIDE AND PREJUDICE
THE RED BADGE OF COURAGE
THE RETURN OF THE NATIVE
ROMEO AND JULIET
THE SCARLET LETTER
SILAS MARNER
A TALE OF TWO CITIES
THE TEMPEST
WUTHERING HEIGHTS